SCIENTIFIC LONDON.

BY

BERNARD H. BECKER.

. . . . . . Juvat integros accedere fontes
Atque haurire.

D. APPLETON & CO., NEW YORK.

1875.

PREFACE.

On becoming a frequent visitor at the meetings of learned Societies, I was astonished to find that the written records of their deeds were few and far between, and that, with the exception of Weld's "History of the Royal Society," but little connected narrative had been produced on a subject of great and increasing interest. Facts of inestimable value lay scattered through endless volumes of "Transactions" and "Proceedings," but these treasures were not arranged in a form accessible to the general reader. According to my lights I have striven, in unambitious fashion, to supply this gap in the literature of science, and in the little book now offered to the public have attempted to describe in a compact form the rise, progress, and present condition of those great Scientific Institutions of which London—and for that matter England—is justly proud.

Both in the collection and arrangement of material for these papers—which originally appeared in the columns of *Iron*—I have received ready and valuable aid from the officers of various institutions, and I take this opportunity of tendering my hearty thanks to Professor Huxley, to Major Donnelly, to Mr. W. Spottiswoode, and to Mr. Henry Cole; to Mr. H. T. Wood and Mr. Davenport, of the Society of Arts; to Mr. Walter White, of the Royal Society; to Mr. Whittall, of the Statistical Society; to Mr. Latimer Clark and Mr. G. E. Preece, of the Society of Telegraph Engineers; to Mr. Trenham Reeks, of the Royal School of Mines; to Mr. Norris, of the Birkbeck Institute; to Mr. H. W. Bates, of the Royal Geographical Society; to Mr. Forrest, of the Institution of Civil Engineers; and especially to Colonel Charles Manby, to whose frequent counsel and friendly supervision I am deeply indebted.

It only remains for me to add that, however much the array of facts in this little volume is due to the courtesy of scientific friends, the only person responsible for the opinions advanced is

THE AUTHOR.

October 10th, 1874.

CONTENTS.

SCIENTIFIC LONDON.

I.

THE ROYAL SOCIETY.

To England belongs the honour of being the first country after Italy to establish a society for the investigation and advancement of physical science. The Royal Society, the most ancient and illustrious of existing scientific bodies, was founded in 1660. The troubles of the great Rebellion were healed—at least for a time—by the restoration of the Stuarts, and the minds of men, relieved for a while from political anxiety, turned with ardour towards the study of science. "The period had arrived when that experimental philosophy to which Bacon had held the torch, and which had already made considerable progress, especially in Italy, was finally established on the ruins of arbitrary figments and partial inductions."

By degrees was formed a group of philosophers who began to knock at the door of truth, "at that door which Newton was destined to force open." These were the founders of the Royal Society.

The road had been admirably prepared by Bacon, and the disciples of the great master of inductive philosophy were not slow in carrying out the plan of a learned society as sketched in the "New Atlantis." Among these were Robert Boyle, Lord Brouncker, Dr. Wallis, Elias Ashmole—who has given his name to a museum at Oxford—the celebrated Oldenburg, and last, but not least, that Christopher Wren who was destined to replace the old Gothic Cathedral of St. Paul's, which, at the period referred to, was the central spot of busy London, by the present noble structure. As early as 1645, and amid all the turmoil of civil war, a few choice spirits had been in the habit of assembling for the purpose of discoursing on experimental philosophy, sometimes at Dr. Goddard's lodgings in Wood Street, and occasionally at the Bull's Head Tavern in Cheapside, where the sacred fire was fanned by the intercourse of kindred spirits, but owing probably to the unsettled condition of public affairs, nothing was done in the way of organizing a learned body.

It chanced, however, that on the 28th November, 1660, several of those who had been in the habit of meeting from time to time were assembled at Gresham College, to hear a lecture on astronomy, by Christopher Wren, who at that time was one of the resident professors at the old Gresham mansion in Bishopsgate. After the lecture a list of names was drawn up, and the number of members fixed at fifty-five. On the 6th March, 1661, the Society proceeded to the election of a president. The choice of the members fell upon Sir Robert Moray, who, according to Burnet, was the life and soul of the institution. Sir Robert being a member of the Privy Council, and in great favour with Charles II., was charged by the king, who, if he never said a foolish thing, certainly did a wise one on this occasion, to assure the growing Society of the royal sympathy and protection. A little more than a year after its foundation the Society was formed into a corporation by royal charter. It was soon found necessary to amend this document, and a second charter was obtained from the king, and sealed on the 22nd of April, 1663. A third charter, conceding to the Royal Society Chelsea College, and some additional privileges, was granted in 1669, but the charter of 1663 is still the fundamental law of the Society. This document declares the king himself to be the founder and patron of the Society, which consists of a president, a council of twenty, and an unlimited number of Fellows. Lord Brouncker was the first president, William Ball the treasurer, John Wilkins and Henry Oldenburg the two secretaries, Sir Robert Moray and the celebrated Boyle members of the council.

Lord Brouncker was at this time Chancellor to the Queen, and had already made himself a name by his mathematical studies. Two remarkable discoveries were made by him. He was the first to introduce continued fractions, and to give a series for the quadrature of a portion of the equilateral hyperbola.

The first meeting of the Council after the concession of the new charter took place on the 13th May, 1663, the Society then consisting of 115 members. By the following November the number had increased to 130, of whom eighteen were noblemen, twenty-two baronets and knights, forty-seven esquires, thirty-two doctors, two bachelors of theology, two masters of arts, and eight were foreigners.

In August, 1663, King Charles II. presented the Royal Society with the mace at present in their possession. This mace—which is made of silver, richly gilt, and weighs 190 oz. avoirdupois—fills an important office in the Society. No meeting can be legally held without it, and the same practice respecting it prevails in the Royal Society as in Parliament. In the House of Commons, when the Speaker is in the chair and the mace on the table, any member may rise to address the House. When the Speaker leaves the chair the mace is taken off the table, and when it is carried out of the building the assembly is no longer a House.

Great interest attaches to the mace of the Royal Society from its having long been supposed to be the identical "bauble" removed by the command of Oliver Cromwell. This, however, has been shown by Mr. Weld to be an erroneous belief. The royal mace used during the reign of Charles I. was broken up with the rest of the crown jewels, and an entirely new mace was made for the Commonwealth. This was ornamented with flowers instead of the cross and ball at the top, with the arms of England and Ireland instead of those of the late king. The mace, still in the possession of the Royal Society, is a truly royal one, consisting of a stem handsomely chased with a running pattern of the thistle, terminated at the upper end by an urn-shaped head surmounted by a crown, ball, and cross. On the head are embossed figures of a rose, harp, thistle, and fleur-de-lys, on each side of which are the letters C. R.

The year 1664 was marked by great activity in the Royal Society. Eight committees were formed for prosecuting researches in different directions. In the month of June Sir John Cutler founded a chair of Mechanics, and, with the consent of the Royal Society, he assigned to the celebrated Hooke a pension of fifty pounds a year, leaving to the Society the care of fixing the number of lectures and their subject. Hooke was also made curator, with a salary of thirty pounds, and apartments were assigned him in Gresham College, where the Society continued to hold its meetings.

On the 6th March, 1665, appeared the first number of "Philosophical Transactions." This report was published by Oldenburg, and submitted to the Council of the Society. During this year the plague proved a serious interruption to the weekly meetings of the Society, and actually compelled Oldenburg to get the seventh and eighth numbers of the "Transactions" printed at Oxford, on account of the impossibility of finding printers in London.

Meetings were held at uncertain intervals until February, 1666. On the 21st of this month the Society met again at Gresham College, under the presidency of Lord Brouncker, and a noteworthy event took place. It was decided that a gift of one hundred pounds made to the Society by Mr. Colwall, should be employed in purchasing a collection of rarities found by Mr. Hubbard. This collection was the nucleus of a museum, which became in time the richest in London. Many presents came to Oldenburg from abroad, the correspondence of this active member having assumed immense proportions. Among the curious objects in this collection was "the skin of a Moor, tanned, with the beard and hair white;" but more worthy of observation was "a clock whose movements are derived from the vicinity of a loadstone," and so adjusted as to "discover the distance of countries at sea by the longitudes." This clock and Hooke's magnetic watch were apparently the pearls of the collection, and the direct ancestors of the electrical clock of the present day.

The great fire of London produced a temporary migration of the Royal Society. It is true that they were not actually burnt out of Gresham College, but that building was seized upon as a temporary Exchange, and the philosophers, elbowed out of the City, found hospitable welcome at Arundel House. Henry Howard, afterwards Duke of Norfolk, not content with putting his house at the disposition of the Society, presented them with a magnificent library, the germ of which was formed by Matthias Corvinus, King of Hungary.

In 1667, at Arundel House, was performed the remarkable experiment of transfusing the blood of a sheep into the veins of a man, the subject of the operation being a poor devil of a student named Arthur Coga, who for the consideration of one guinea of the lawful money of the realm consented to lose eight ounces of his own blood and receive into his veins fourteen ounces of sheep's blood. Pepys saw this Coga at a tavern, and describes him "as a little frantic, a poor debauched man." The experiment, if *in corpore vili*, was attended with no evil consequences to the patient, which is more than could be said for the Continental experiments made about the same time, which caused the death of sundry persons, and brought the transfusion of blood into complete discredit. The mechanical science of the Society found ample recognition at Court, Catharine of Braganza requesting this learned body to produce for her use a thermometer, which was duly made by Hooke.

The year 1671 was marked by the rise of the greatest luminary of the Royal Society. A young candidate was proposed for the honour of fellowship, one Isaac Newton, professor of mathematics at the University of Cambridge. Newton had already made his mark, having invented the reflecting telescope. The actual instrument constructed by his own hands is now in the possession of the Royal Society, and is justly esteemed one of its most precious relics. Newton was elected on the 11th of January, 1672, and on the 8th of February communicated to the Society his researches into the nature of light. The publication of these inquiries in the "Transactions" aroused a storm of opposition.

Hooke in England, and Huyghens abroad, attacked

not only his conclusions, but the accuracy of the experiments on which they were based. Although much harassed by the controversy, Newton replied within a few months in a manner which firmly established his general doctrines.

Among the secretaries of this period figures the name of John Evelyn, and among the foreign correspondents the celebrated Leuwenhoeck, in whose hands the microscope finally became a useful scientific instrument. Leuwenhoeck not only transmitted his valuable observations to the Royal Society, but bequeathed to that body twenty-six microscopes, the glasses of which he had polished himself.

Great names now appear on the roll. Flamsteed, a Fellow of the Society, was appointed astronomical observer at Greenwich. Two years later Edmund Halley was also elected a Fellow on his return from St. Helena, where he had been observing the stars of the Southern hemisphere. In 1684 Dr. Denis Papin—the inventor of the famous Digester—was named curator, on condition of making an experiment at every general meeting of the Society; and the year is also remarkable as that in which Samuel Pepys was elected president. Of no "considerable" family, being actually the son of a tailor, this remarkable man and delightful gossip was educated at St. Paul's School, and at Trinity College, Cambridge, where he left no particular mark. In 1655, when only twenty-three years of age, he married a girl of fifteen, to whose family connections he possibly owed part of his advancement. Twenty-nine years later he took his seat as president of the Royal Society.

No date is more justly celebrated in the annals of this august Society than that of the 28th of April, 1686. At the ordinary meeting held on that day, Dr. Vincent presented the manuscript of the first book of the immortal work of Newton, "Philosophiæ Naturalis Principia Mathematica." The Society wished to print, at its own expense, the work which was dedicated to it, but the finances of the institution had been so terribly depleted by the publication of Willoughby's "De Historiâ Piscium," that even the salaries of the regular officers were in arrear. Members did not pay their subscriptions, and some of them, like Newton, were specially exempted from payment of the yearly fifty-two shillings, on account of the inadequacy of their means. Finally, Halley took the risk of publishing the "Principia" on his own shoulders, a deed sufficient to immortalize him had he done nothing further for the advancement of science.

When it is remembered that the volume contained sixty-four sheets, and above a hundred diagrams cut in wood, it is wonderful that Halley should have performed the laborious task of editing it in about six months. Halley's troubles were added to very considerably by the reluctance of Newton to publish the third book of the "Principia"—"De Systemate Mundi." Hooke, perhaps the greatest mechanical genius of his own or any other age, felt himself outraged by Newton having omitted in his preface all mention of him. Halley writes to Newton in May, 1686, that "Mr. Hooke has some pretensions upon the invention of the rule of decrease of gravity being reciprocally as the squares of the distances from the centre. He says you had the notion from him, though he owns the demonstration of the curves generated thereby to be wholly your own. How much of this is so you know best, as likewise what you have to do in this matter." In reply to this Newton declared his intention to suppress the third book altogether, and said, "Philosophy is such an impertinently litigious lady that a man had as good be engaged in lawsuits as have to do with her. I found it so formerly, and now I am no sooner come near her again than she gives me warning." Halley's invincible arguments and entreaties fortunately prevailed on Newton not to suppress the third book.

The entire work was written by Newton in about a year and a half, and was, as we have seen, hurried through the press by the indefatigable Halley. It is depressing to find that the circulation of the first edition was undoubtedly small, inasmuch as in 1692, when the reputation of the "Principia" was established, Huyghens, who was anxious for a second edition, was of opinion that two hundred copies would suffice. The volume contains the dedication to the Royal Society, a brief preface, verses by Halley in honour of Newton, definitions, axioms, a short book on unresisted motion, a second on resisted motion, and a third on the system of the universe. "Halley's verses," says Mr. Weld in his "History of the Royal Society," "were somewhat altered by Bentley in the second edition, but the original readings were very nearly restored in the third." The publication of the "Principia" was licensed by the Royal Society on the 30th June, 1686, and the *imprimatur* signed by the ubiquitous Samuel Pepys, is dated on the fifth of the following month.

The manuscript of the immortal "Principia," entirely written by Newton's own hand, is in admirable preservation, and is justly considered the greatest treasure in the possession of the Royal Society.

In the years 1687-88-89, numerous important inventions were presented to the Society by Hooke, Halley, and Papin—Hooke especially pursuing his astronomical investigations with a huge telescope mounted at Gresham College.

On the 14th June, 1699, was exhibited to the Society

a model of Savery's condensing steam-engine. In the minutes it is recorded that "Mr. Savery entertained the Society with showing his engine to raise water by the force of fire. He was thanked for showing the experiment, which succeeded according to expectation, and was approved of." Savery presented the Society with a drawing of his engine, still preserved among the Society's collection of prints and drawings, and entitled, "An Engine for Raising Water by Fire," by Thomas Savery. Doubtless Savery had a predecessor in the history of steam, but it will be remembered that although the Marquis of Worcester invented the steam-engine "to drive up water by fire," seen by Cosmo de Medici, Grand Duke of Tuscany, in operation at Vauxhall in 1656, we are indebted to Savery for the introduction of a vacuum which enabled his engine to perform double the work of that invented by the Marquis of Worcester.

On the 11th February, 1708, Newton then being President of the Royal Society, a proposition was submitted "concerning a new-invented boat to be rowed with oars moved by heat." At the two ensuing meetings the matter was again brought forward, accompanied by letters of recommendation from Leibnitz. Papin says that, inasmuch as "it is certain that it is a thing of great consequence to be able to apply the force of fire for to save the labour of men," and that "the Parliament of England granted some years ago a patent to Esquire Savery for an engine he had invented for that purpose, and his Highness Charles, Landgrave of Hesse, hath also caused several costly experiments for the same design," he therefore offers with all dutiful respect "to make here an engine after the manner that has been practised at Cassell, and to fit it so that it may be applied for the moving of ships." Dr. Papin wished much to make "the said Cassellian engine at his own cost," but was unable to furnish the necessary funds. The Royal Society was unfortunately in a similar position.

Papin clearly saw that ships might be propelled by paddles moved by steam. In a paper published as early as 1690 in the "Acta Eruditorum," he says, "Without doubt oars fixed to an axis could be made most conveniently to revolve by our tubes. It would only be necessary to furnish the piston-rod with teeth, which might act on a toothed wheel properly fitted to it, and which, being fixed on the axis to which the oars were attached, would communicate a rotary motion to it."

Despite the squabbles between Newton and Flamsteed, the Royal Society waxed mighty under the presidency of the author of the "Principia." On the death of Sir Godfrey Copley, in 1709, the interest of one hundred pounds became vested in the Society.

For awhile this sum was given to the curator to pay the expenses of experiments, but was finally employed in striking a gold medal of the value of five pounds, to be given to the author of the best experiment made during the year. This medal is the greatest honour at the disposal of the Royal Society. It has been given for a century and a quarter to the authors of the most brilliant discoveries made in England and on the continent of Europe. The first Copley medal was awarded to Stephen Gray—a name almost forgotten until Dr. Richardson, only the other day, vindicated the claim of the first Copley medallist to the title of father of electrical science. Among the medallists are found the names of Benjamin Franklin, James Bradley, John Dollond, and John Smeaton, of Cavendish, Priestley, Maskelyne, Hutton, Hunter, Rumford, Volta, Attwood, Astley Cooper, Wollaston, Davy, Brodie, Brande, Brewster, Buckland, Arago, Faraday and Leibig, Herschel and Leverrier.

Towards the middle of the last century the Royal Society took an active part in promoting the change of style effected in England on the 2nd of September, 1752. A few years later active measures were taken for observing the transit of Venus, which, according to the prediction of Halley, was to occur in 1761. The importance of this event in determining the exact distance of the sun from the earth induced the treasury to give £1600 for the expedition to St. Helena conducted by Nevil Maskelyne, but bad weather interfered with the success of the observation. This loss, however, was recovered eight years later, when Messrs. Green and Banks (afterwards Sir Joseph) sailed for Tahiti with Captain Cook in the *Endeavour*, and obtained their observations on a cloudless day.

The year 1784 was marked by a grand discovery—that of the composition of water, attributed by some to Cavendish and by others to Watt. Doctors disagree severely on this vexed question. It will suffice to remark that Arago, Dumas, and Berzelius favour the claims of Watt, while Whewell, Peacock, and Brown rule for Cavendish.

The early part of the present century was marked in the Royal Society by the advent of Sir Humphrey Davy. In 1806 he read his celebrated paper "On some Chemical Agencies." "This," says Whewell, "was a great event, perhaps the greatest event of the epoch." Although the war between England and France was at its height, Davy's work was crowned by the Institute of France, and the author was presented with a prize of three thousand francs. Davy now devoted his attention to the illumination of mines, and discovered the safety lamp, the originality of which was, as appears to have been the case with almost every scientific invention, contested at the time.

Nevertheless, the honours of discovery were awarded to Davy by a committee of the Royal Society, and the colliery proprietors presented him with a service of plate valued at £2500. In addition to this solid reward all the honours of the Royal Society were showered upon the illustrious chemist. He received the Copley medal, the Rumford medal, delivered the Baker Lecture several times, and in 1820 took his seat as president in the chair whilom occupied by Wren, Newton, Sloane, and Banks. From its foundation to the present time the Royal Society has thus numbered many illustrious names among its presidents, from Lord Brouncker to Dr. Hooker, and during the two centuries of its existence has occupied various dwellings—Gresham College, then Arundel House, then Gresham College again, then a house in Crane Court, then Somerset House, and lastly, after many migrations, has found a home at Burlington House, the handsome building extending from Burlington Gardens to Piccadilly. The Society receives house room, but nothing beyond that, from the Government of the country, being now, as always, an entirely self-supporting institution. It is true that a thousand pounds a year are voted for the encouragement of original research; but the Royal Society only advise the Ministry of the day as to the manner in which this sum should be employed. A Special Committee of the Society is appointed to recommend the method of distributing this fund, but no portion of it finds its way into the coffers of the Society.

Rooms are also provided in the wings of Burlington House for the Society of Antiquaries, the Linnæan Society, the Geological Society, the Royal Astronomical Society, and the Chemical Society. The Royal Society has on the first floor a handsome suite of reception-rooms—available for the annual *soirées* of the president—and a library affording space for 35,000 volumes. On the ground floor is a hall, an ante-room, and the room in which the Society holds its meetings. These take place once in every week from the third Thursday in November to the third Thursday in June. A record of these meetings is preserved in the octavo "Proceedings," and the best papers are printed in the quarto "Transactions." These last have been regularly printed since their institution in 1665, the series now extending to 160 volumes.

The Society has at its disposal four medals by which to mark its appreciation of scientific investigations and remarkable discoveries. The first award of the Copley medal was made in 1731, and of the Rumford medal in 1800, to the founder himself, Benjamin Count Rumford, for his various discoveries in respect of light and heat. In the year 1825

George IV. communicated through Sir Robert Peel his intention "to found two gold medals of the value of fifty guineas each, to be awarded as honorary premiums under the direction of the President and Council of the Royal Society, in such manner as shall by the excitement of competition among men of science seem best calculated to promote the objects for which the Royal Society was instituted." The two first medals were awarded in 1826 to John Dalton and James Ivory. William IV. and her present Majesty have continued the gift of these Royal medals, and they are therefore annually awarded. The total number of Fellows, including foreign members (limited to fifty), is now 571.

Besides the mace already mentioned, and the reflecting telescope made by Newton, the Society's treasures include the sun-dial cut by the great philosopher, when a boy, in the wall of his father's house, and a large collection of the portraits of Presidents, distinguished Fellows, and other great luminaries of science, painted by Van Somer, Sir Peter Lely, Sir Godfrey Kneller, Sir Joshua Reynolds, Sir Thomas Lawrence, and other great artists.

These pictures are dispersed throughout the rooms occupied by the Society. On the first floor one of the most remarkable portraits is that of Copernicus, who, after travelling over Europe, studying astronomy at

Bologna, and filling the Chair of Mathematics at Rome, settled down in his quiet canonry at Frauenburg, and at length embodied the result of his labours in the celebrated treatise, "De Orbium Cœlestium Revolutionibus," to the publication of which he only consented a short time before his death—having probably a keen presentiment that the Copernican system would cost him his canonry, if not his life. The clean-shaven, priestly face is certainly a remarkable one, with the long upper lip and portentously long, sharp chin, so often found in men of genius. Near him hangs George Buchanan, a bald and grizzly-bearded Scot, looking mighty solemn at the neighbourhood of that bright black-haired Frenchman, Descartes. Not far from these worthies may be seen the portrait of Flamsteed—the first Royal "Astronomical Observator," to whom mankind is indebted for that enormous mass of astronomical observations which furnished the first trustworthy account of the fixed stars. The harsh, rugged features of Galileo next arrest attention, and after contemplating his worn face the eye rests complacently on the picture of Dr. Bradley, whilom Astronomer Royal, and the very *beau idéal* of a prosperous Churchman. Enthroned in an attitude of tremendous dignity, Edmund Halley looms on the wall—a don every inch of him, but an industrious secretary withal, and the composer of no less than eighty-one papers, published in "Philosophical Transactions," on subjects connected with optics, mechanics, mathematics, astronomy, magnetism, the law of mortality, &c. The great Hobbes looks every inch a Puritan, albeit his works enjoyed in his own day a very similar reputation to those of Strauss in our own time. John Locke, his great successor, appears in an admirable picture by Kneller, and John Evelyn looks sadly forth from Kerseboom's canvas. The effect of gazing upon this galaxy of worthies is an inexpressible feeling of smallness in the gazer, who is glad to change the scene and descend to the ante-room, where he is restored to a more comfortable frame of mind by the contemplation of the gracious features of his Majesty King Charles II., the amiable, if erring, monarch, who apologized to his courtiers for being such an "unconscionable time in dying." The portrait by Lely depicts the jovial monarch in anything but evil case. The large eyes and drooping eyelashes give a thoughtful look to a face which, were it not for the bright scarlet over-full underlip, might well be taken for that of a philosopher. In one feature—the long nose—the kingly countenance is quite in keeping with the scientific visages ranged around—a preponderance of nose being remarkably characteristic of great thinkers—Newton, Locke, Boyle, and many others being gifted with an enormous quantity of that useful organ. So well was the necessity for an important nose recognized by Tycho Brahe, that that great astronomer, having had the misfortune to lose a portion of his in a duel, supplied the loss by an artificial nose made of gold, so well-formed and coloured as to be hardly distinguishable, it is said, from the natural feature. In his portrait, however, the nose of Tycho Brahe looks odd enough, and gives a singular expression to a countenance finished off by a pointed beard, and adorned with a pair of portentous moustaches. Near the portrait of the Royal founder hang the pictures of the late Duke of Sussex and of Earl Rosse, the builder of the famous telescope.

On entering the large room, the well-known features of Newton are discovered in the central place of honour, over the chair occupied by the president. On the right of Newton is the sad, weary-looking countenance of Robert Boyle, and the handsome features of that genial-looking cavalier, Lord Brouncker. Farther on is descried the dark *bourgeois* face of our old friend Samuel Pepys,—almost smothered in a tremendous full-bottomed wig,—near whom looms large the Johnsonian figure of Sir Joseph Banks, adorned with the star and riband of the Bath. Here is Sir Christopher Wren, also much bewigged, turning his back on St. Paul's, and there, in all the glory of tights and Hessians, the figure of Dr. Wollaston, rendered famous by his researches into electricity and galvanism, and rich by his discovery of the method of making platinum malleable. A sense of awe again creeps over the visitor as he contemplates the massive heads which have contributed so much to the well-being of mankind.

It will be seen that a visit to the halls of the Royal Society is not an expedition to be undertaken lightly, or in an irreverent spirit. He who seeks to be admitted to the sacred *penetralia*, where science sits enthroned among her chosen votaries, feels very much as he did on his first visit to the House of Lords, an institution which has much in common with the Royal Society. The would-be visitor must first look up a friendly F.R.S., who, if the applicant be deemed worthy, will introduce him either personally or by letter to the acting secretary, Mr. White, who will enter his name on the book, bracketed with the name of the introducer, and he will now only have to present himself at the fashionable hour of 8.30 to be at once admitted to the Upper House of Science.

Having fulfilled these conditions, I presented myself at Burlington House on one of those foggy evenings for which London is recovering its ancient notoriety. Having deposited my coat and hat with a careful attendant, I found myself in the spacious ante-room, gazing on the dark features of his Majesty King Charles II., who, albeit of an over gay and festive turn of mind, had probably acquired a certain *dilettante* taste for science from his dashing relative, that ringleted Prince of Bohemia, who—equal to either fortune—led a charge of cavalry in the field, or conducted a scientific experiment in the quiet recesses of his laboratory with equal success. This same "Rupert's drop," the scientific toy destined to immortalize its inventor, affords grave matter for reflection to those endowed with a philosophic temperament. The heroes of Long Marston Moor and Naseby, dashing Cavaliers and sturdy Roundheads, have long since rendered back to earth the strength which they drew from her mighty bosom. As the world whirls on their names will wax dim enough in the page of history, but "Rupert of the Rhine" has written his name in indelible characters on the records of scientific discovery.

The members are now dropping in one by one, and are chatting pleasantly in groups, or examining specimens and photographs of curious organisms brought by a distinguished Fellow, who is the happy possessor of a sun-picture of the gigantic octopus recently washed ashore at Newfoundland. Thoughtful-looking, grey-haired men are the majority of the F.R.S., but active withal, and evidently men to whom hard work and constant study have become necessary stimulants. For the nonce they put on a holiday air, as if bent on enjoying a little bit of scientific dissipation, and resolved to make a scientific night of it. But the clock points to half-past eight, the hour at which proceedings commence, and punctually to the moment the audience settle down here and there, while the president proceeds to take the chair.

On a dais placed immediately beneath the portrait of Newton, at the upper end of the room, sits the president, enthroned in a massive chair, evidently made "on the lines" of Sir Joseph Banks, and affording ample room for Dr. Hooker, whose spare figure and study-worn face are surmounted by a pair of those bushy eyebrows which so frequently add force and character to the features of those deeply learned in the law and those other sciences to which Mr. Ayrton recently declined to concede any priority over jurisprudence. Before the president lies the mace, without which no regular meeting can be held. On his right sits Professor Stokes, Lucasian Professor of Mathematics, the senior secretary, and on his left sits, or rather reclines in his armchair, one who has done much to gild the pill of science and make it acceptable to the many—Professor Huxley. A short paper is read in the absence of the contributor by the junior secretary, and duly committed to the archives of the Society, after which ceremony the meaning of some complicated clockwork on the table is made manifest. The inventor of the instrument—Professor Roscoe—steps up to the table at the invitation of the president, and explains the machine in question, a clever contrivance for measuring automatically the strength of the actinic rays of the sun, by means of a roll of sensitive papers, successive portions of which are unwound, exposed to the light for a certain time, and reeled off, thus preserving a record of the intensity of the chemical rays during various periods of the day. At the conclusion of the exposition, the president invites discussion, and the Fellows, nothing loth, attack the subject vigorously. The reader of the paper having replied to the objections brought forward, is formally thanked by the Society, and his invention duly recorded in the archives. Another paper is read on Explosive Compounds, the conductivity of concussion by rough and polished tubes, and more especially on the extraordinary power of water in transmitting the shock of an explosion to an immense distance. This subject provokes a lengthened and lively discussion, at the conclusion of which the meeting comes to an end; the chairman rises, the mace is removed, and the learned Fellows abandon themselves to tea and scientific gossip.

II.

THE ROYAL INSTITUTION.

THAT stronghold of fashionable science, the Royal Institution in Albemarle Street, covers a site of great historical interest. In 1665, when the space now occupied by Arlington Street was taken up by the gardens of Goring House, three stately villas were in course of erection on the opposite or north side of Piccadilly. Between Burlington House on the east—built originally by the Sir John Denham who poisoned his beautiful wife—and Berkeley House on the west, the entire space was occupied by the stately mansion built by Lord Chancellor Clarendon. Pepys, of course, went to see it while building, and has a prime bit of scandal: "the common people have already called it Dunkirk House, from their opinion of his having a good bribe for the selling of that town." John Evelyn—a partial critic, inasmuch as he had had a hand in its internal adornment as well as in laying out the gardens—declared that he had "never seen a nobler pile" than that occupied by Lord Clarendon until his flight after he had been deprived of the great seal. It was a short-lived palace. The Chancellor dying in exile, the Earl, his successor, sold "that which cost £50,000 building to the young Duke of Albemarle for £25,000, and ultimately this stately palace," says Evelyn, was "decreed to ruin, to support the prodigious waste the Duke of Albemarle had made of his estate since the old man died." He sold it to the highest bidder, and it fell to "certain rich bankers and mechanics, who gave for it and the ground about it £35,000; they design a new town, as it were, and a most magnificent piazza. 'Tis said they have already materials towards it, with what they sold of the house, alone more worth than what they paid for it. See the vicissitude of earthly things! I was astonished at the demolition, nor less at the little army of labourers and artificers levelling the ground and contriving great buildings, at an expense of £200,000 if they perfect their design." Bond Street, Dover Street, and Albemarle Street were the result of the venture of the "bankers and mechanics," who were shrewd enough to descry, more than two hundred years ago, that cities follow the sun and march westward.

Commencing with the nineteenth century, the Royal Institution can claim for itself many of the most remarkable discoveries which have distinguished an era of unrivalled activity. It owes its origin partly to Sir Joseph Banks, but in a far greater degree to a more remarkable man. Benjamin Thompson, afterwards Count Rumford, was a lineal descendant of one James Thompson, who figured at Charlestown in Winthrop's company in 1630. Born in his grandfather's farmhouse, he enjoyed the advantage of a good grammar-school education, and then advanced in the world by the steps familiar to this day in America, but almost unknown in Europe. He was apprenticed to an importer of British goods, was allowed to make small ventures on his own account, fancied that he had invented perpetual motion, took a great interest in questions relating to light, heat, and the wind, lost his place, and blew himself up with fireworks before the age of sixteen. At seventeen he was a dry-goods clerk in Boston, studied French during his evenings, and got himself an electrical machine with money earned by cutting and carting firewood. He then boarded for some eighteen months with a Dr. John Hay, and picked up a little anatomy, chemistry, surgery, and physic, and in 1771 went to Cambridge, Massachusetts, to attend Winthrop's lectures on Experimental Philosophy. He then, after the manner of his country, "taught school" at Wilmington; and afterwards became master of a school at a place originally called Rumford, but afterwards re-christened Concord, when the disputes as to the State to which it belonged were finally settled, and it was ceded to New Hampshire for good and all.

Shortly before attaining the age of twenty, Thompson, a fine, handsome young man, married—or, to use his own expression—"was married by" Mrs. Rolfe, a wealthy widow of Concord. There was now no more occasion to "teach school," and Thompson hoped for leisure to pursue science vigorously; but the American Revolution breaking out, he speedily found his way to England, in 1778 was elected a Fellow of the Royal Society, and two years later became an Under Secretary of State, and Colonel of the King's American Dragoons. At the conclusion of the war he was knighted by George the Third, and, having met the Elector of Bavaria at Strasbourg, passed a considerable time in Munich, busying himself in improving the breed of cattle and in building workhouses, and it was in order to find the most economical method of lighting the workhouse in Munich that he initiated the series of experiments afterwards embodied in a paper on "The Relative Intensities of the Light emitted by Luminous Bodies," read before the Royal Society.

Honours now fell thickly upon the successful American. In 1785 he was elected member of the

Bavarian Academy of Sciences, and in the two succeeding years was made a member of the Berlin Academy of Sciences and received the order of St. Stanislaus. Finally, Sir Benjamin Thompson became Lieutenant-General of the Bavarian Armies, received the order of the White Eagle, and was made a Count of the Holy Roman Empire.

After the death of his wife he travelled for sixteen months in Italy, and during his stay at Verona rebuilt the kitchens of the two great hospitals—La Pieta and La Misericordia. Seven-eighths of the firewood were saved, and his success in this enterprise appears to have greatly encouraged Count Rumford to pursue his investigations into the proper management of fuel. A curious essay written by him about this time contains the mixed philanthropic and philosophic germ of the Royal Institution. This is a "proposal for forming in London, by private subscription, an establishment for feeding the poor and giving them useful employment, and also for furnishing food at a cheap rate to others who may stand in need of such assistance, connected with an institution for introducing and bringing forward into general use new inventions and improvements, particularly such as relate to the management of heat and the saving of fuel, and to various other mechanical contrivances by which domestic comfort and economy may be promoted." This was followed by other essays on "Food and Feeding the Poor," on "Rumford Soup and Soup Kitchens," and on "Chimney Fireplaces." The Rumford medal was now presented to the Royal Society "for discoveries tending to improve the theories of fire, of heat, of light, and of colours, and to new inventions and contrivances by which the generation and preservation and management of heat and of light may be preserved." The endowment of the medal consisted of £1000 stock, and was, I may add, presented on the first award, in 1802, to its founder. Meanwhile Rumford went to Ireland and fitted up laundries and model kitchens, cottage fireplaces, and model lime-kilns; served in Bavaria, preserving by his firmness and skill the neutrality of that country; and finally determined to return to America, but was deterred from carrying out this project by his anxiety to launch the Royal Institution. In the mind of Rumford the dominant idea was originally that of bettering the condition and increasing the comforts of the poor. A society was formed for this purpose, and out of it sprang, from a proposal of Count Rumford, a scheme for forming a new "Establishment in London for Diffusing the Knowledge of Useful Mechanical Improvements." The two great objects of the institution were declared to be the diffusion of the knowledge aforesaid, and the teaching of the application of scientific discoveries to the improvement of arts and manufactures in this country. To fulfil the first object were to be exhibited full-sized working models of fire-places, kitchens, stoves, grates, boilers, coppers, &c., and smaller models of houses, bridges, spinning-wheels, and of all "such other machinery and useful instruments as the managers of the institution shall deem worthy of the public notice."

In order to carry into effect the second object of this institution—namely, "teaching the application of science to the useful purposes of life"—a lecture-room was to be fitted up "for philosophical lectures and experiments, and a complete laboratory and philosophical apparatus, with the necessary instruments, will be provided for making chemical and other philosophical experiments." On the 7th March, 1779, a meeting was held at the house of Sir Joseph Banks, at which the list of original fifty-four proprietors and subscribers of fifty guineas was read. In addition to the names of Rumford and Banks are found on this list those of Angerstein, Joseph Grote, the Duke of Devonshire, Earl Spencer, Earl Holland, Lord Palmerston, the Earl of Winchelsea, and William Wilberforce. By the end of June, 1801, the Royal Institution had received upwards of twenty thousand pounds in subscriptions. The site of four houses had been purchased in Albemarle Street, professors of chemistry, physics, and mechanics had been engaged, daily lectures were delivered, a spacious chemical laboratory had been erected, workshops for making models had been built, and skilled workmen engaged for making apparatus and models of various kinds. Early in this year Count Rumford wrote to his daughter that the Royal Institution was "not only the fashion but the rage," and mentions incidentally that "we have found a nice, able man for this place as lecturer—Humphry Davy." This "nice, able man" was the eminent philosopher destined to explode a great part of Rumford's scheme, his models, his fire-places, his kitchens, his experimental cooking, and his experimental dinners. In 1802 Count Rumford forsook England for Bavaria—as it turned out, for ever—and, like many other benefactors of his species, was considered a good riddance. So far as can be ascertained, the American-Bavarian Count was offensively dictatorial in his manner, and exasperated those whom he did not succeed in crushing. Having shaken off Dr. Garnett, the first professor of chemistry at the Royal Institution, he engaged Davy as an assistant lecturer in chemistry, director of the laboratory, and assistant editor of the journals of the Institution. The future president of the Royal Society was granted a room in the house, coals, candles, and a salary of 100 guineas per annum.

The first interview of Davy with Count Rumford was not very agreeable to the young chemist, then in his twenty-third year. The intensely juvenile air of the candidate, his almost provincial manners, and a slight Cornwall accent, sufficed to reduce the glacial Count to a lower temperature than usual. With considerable difficulty Davy obtained permission to give a few lectures on the properties of gases. This, however, was sufficient. At the first lecture the variety and ingenious combination of his ideas, and the fire, vivacity, clearness, and novelty with which they were expounded, enchanted the few who came to listen to the young lecturer, in whom they found united the power of poetry, oratory, and philosophy. The second lecture was crowded, and his course was obliged to be removed to the large amphitheatre, whither his fervid genius, and in some degree his youth and good looks, drew immense audiences. The ladies were charmed by the handsome young lecturer, and never tired of praising the beauty of his eyes, which they declared were "made for something besides poring over crucibles."

Before coming to the Royal Institution, Davy had already attained a certain celebrity by discovering the anæsthetic properties of nitrous oxide, and the period of his professorship was signalized by many brilliant discoveries. Named titular professor of chemistry in 1802, he only resigned the chair in 1813. He delivered his last lecture on the 9th April, 1812, the day after he was knighted by the Prince Regent, and the day before his marriage with Mrs. Apreece, a wedding which put him in possession of a large fortune. The splendour shed upon the Royal Institution by the new professor of chemistry prevented the exhibition of any regret at the entire alteration of the original plan of the establishment. The Institution was no longer a popular school of technical science, but became almost the exclusive property of the higher classes. Ladies of the highest rank, and young noblemen, assiduously followed the lectures of Davy, while his researches in the laboratory produced the most solid results. It was there that he discovered the laws of electro-chemical decomposition, and succeeded in decomposing fixed alkalis—that he established the true nature of chlorine and the philosophy of flame. The electric battery with which the separation of potassium and sodium was operated is still preserved in the Royal Institution along with other apparatus used by Davy. The delight of the investigator, on seeing the globules of the new metal start through the crust of potash and catch fire on contact with the air, was intense. "He could not contain his joy, and danced round the room in an ecstatic transport; it was only after a while that he recovered sufficient calmness to continue the experiment." An immense electric battery was now constructed, and this heavy artillery directed against resisting earths. The result of experiment was to add four new metals to the list—barium, strontium, calcium, and magnesium. On resigning the chair of chemistry, Davy declared that he only renounced teaching in order to devote himself to original investigation, but after this date his life was only marked by one great discovery—that of the safety-lamp which bears his name.

In the year marked by the rising of that brilliant star, Sir Humphry Davy, the directors of the Royal Institution made another great success by appointing to the chair of natural philosophy a man of transcendant genius, the celebrated Dr. Young. He was one of the few infant prodigies who have made a mark in after-life. At two years of age he could read. At four he could recite by heart numerous English and Latin poems, of which last, by the way, he did not then understand a word; but by the age of fourteen he had learned—besides Greek and Latin—French, Italian, Hebrew, Persian, and Arabic. His passion for learning was immense, and his talent for overcoming difficulties astounding. On reaching man's estate he was an accomplished linguist, a brilliant mathematician, a botanist, a skilful musician, a neat turner, and a daring circus rider. This universal genius did not remain long at the Royal Institution, but yet had time to deliver a notable course of lectures on Natural Philosophy before his retirement, when his place was occupied by Dalton. The famous author of the Atomic Theory was surprised, like other people, at the youthful appearance of Davy, and writes, characteristically enough:—"He is a very agreeable and very intelligent young man, and we have extremely interesting conversations of an evening; his principal defect—as a philosopher—is that he does not smoke."

Although in the foremost rank of scientific men, Dalton was far from achieving great success as a lecturer, being almost utterly devoid of the fluency and power of illustration possessed in such a remarkable degree by Davy and Faraday. A most amusing account was given by Babbage of the incidents attending the presentation of Dalton at Court. Firstly, he was a Quaker, and would not wear the sword, which is an indispensable appendage of ordinary Court dress. Secondly, the robe of a Doctor of Civil Law was known to be objectionable on account of its colour—scarlet—one forbidden to Quakers. Luckily, it was recollected that Dalton was afflicted with the peculiar colour-blindness which bears his name, and that, as the cherries and the leaves of a cherry-tree were to him of the same colour, the scarlet gown would present to him no extraordinary appearance. So perfect, indeed, was the colour-blindness, that this most modest and simple of men, whose only pleasures were a pipe and a game of bowls, after having received the doctor's gown at Oxford, actually wore it for several days in happy unconsciousness of the effect he produced in the streets. The inventor of the calculating machine, having offered to present his Quaker friend, was evidently in a state of fussy excitement about the result of the experiment. Poor Dalton was compelled to rehearse thoroughly the ceremony of presentation by the inexorable calculator, who—having found the chances in favour of a *faux-pas* to preponderate—was in a dreadful "taking" on the eventful day. The calculator was completely wrong. The King addressed a few remarks to Dalton, who replied in fitting terms, and the tribulation of Babbage was over.

While the claims of science were amply supplied by the genius of Dalton, Young, and Davy, literature and moral philosophy were entrusted to no ordinary hands. During the years 1804-5-6, the town-talk of London was divided between Young Roscius, the youthful tragedian, and the lectures on moral philosophy delivered by the Rev. Sydney Smith, who, forty years after, said, "I did not know a word about moral philosophy, but wanted two hundred pounds to furnish my house. My success was prodigious." The "loudest wit I e'er was deafened with" probably exaggerated his ignorance of his subject, as he had passed five years at Edinburgh, and had opportunities of hearing Dugald Stuart and Thomas Brown; but in any case the lectures were a certain success in the hands of the eloquent preacher, who, if himself knowing little about moral philosophy, addressed an audience which knew nothing at all. Of very different calibre were the lectures on poetry delivered by Coleridge. It will be recollected that it was in these famous discourses that the author of "Christabel" promulgated those views which have since spread far and wide, and will probably hold their ground when the ephemeral opponents of Shakspeare, and worshippers of a second-rate poet like Schiller, have for long ages been consigned to oblivion.

On the retirement of Davy, in 1813, William Thomas Brand, a distinguished chemist and Copley medallist, was nominated to the chair, which he so admirably filled for forty years. Meanwhile, a young man whose achievements were destined to invest the Royal Institution with peculiar glory had, in a manner of speaking, received the mantle of Davy. Michael Faraday was born at Newington Butts, of poor parents. His father was a farrier, of whom—to the great sorrow of Professor Tyndall—his son could never call to mind a single trait of intelligence. The boy was apprenticed to a bookbinder, but in his leisure moments learnt "a little chemistry and other parts of philosophy." He had so far advanced as to construct for himself an electrical machine, when his master happened to show this specimen of ingenuity to one of his clients, Mr. Dance, who obtained permission for the apprentice bookbinder to be present at the four last lectures of Davy. The youth listened attentively, and made such notes that he was enabled to write a report of the lectures, which he sent to Davy, with a modest request that he might be employed in the laboratory of the Institution. Davy was struck by the clearness and exactitude of the young bookbinder, and gave him, at the commencement of 1813, the post of laboratory assistant. Towards the end of the year he accompanied Davy abroad, as his assistant and secretary. Returning to London in 1815, he recommenced his duties in the laboratory of the Institution, was appointed Director of the Laboratory in 1825, and two years later became one of the regular professors of the Institution, where his scientific researches, like those of Davy, were made at the cost of the Society alone, without any assistance on the part of the State.

The creed of this great philosopher, who had the glory of holding aloft among the nations the scientific name of England for a period of forty years, is thus clearly and briefly expressed:—"I have long held an opinion, almost amounting to conviction, in common, I believe, with many other lovers of natural knowledge, that the various forms under which the forces of matter are made manifest have one common origin —in other words, are so directly related and mutually dependent, that they are convertible, as it were, into one another, and possess equivalents of power in their action." This is what Professor Tyndall, in his *éloge* of "Faraday as a Discoverer," proclaims as the jewel contained in the famous paper "On the Magnetization of Light, and the Illumination of the Lines of Magnetic Force." The same eloquent expositor does ample justice to the prophetic element in Faraday's intellect:—"Faraday was more than a philosopher, and often wrought by an inspiration to be understood by sympathy alone. The prophetic element in his character occasionally coloured, and even injured (?) the utterance of the man of science; but, subtracting that element—though you might have conferred on him intellectual symmetry—you would have destroyed his motive force."

Among the many achievements of Faraday are the demonstration of the condensibility of many gases and his investigations into the reciprocal relations of heat, light, magnetism, and electricity. Not the least noble quality of this remarkable man was his marked preference of a purely scientific career over the acquirement of wealth. With the reputation acquired by the year 1832, he might have made several thousands a year by ordinary professional work, but considering all the time not actually devoted to experiment or to demonstration as a sacrifice of original investigation, Faraday lived and died poor in the world's goods.

At the present day the Royal Institution maintains its renown—thanks to Professor Tyndall, who, by his work on "Heat Considered as a Mode of Motion," has proved himself no unworthy successor of Davy and Faraday. The late President, Sir Henry Holland, *clarum et venerabile nomen*, was, on his decease, replaced by the Duke of Northumberland, whose keen interest in scientific inquiry is well known. The important office of Treasurer and Honorary Secretary—on which to a great extent the success of the Institution depends—is now ably filled by Mr. W. Spottiswoode.

The Royal Institution, in addition to the attractions of its lectures, possesses a model-room, a newspaper-room, a reading-room, and a library of 36,000 volumes, presided over by Mr. Benjamin Vincent.

As might be expected in a highly-fashionable institution, membership is not acquired at a cheap rate, but candidates who are proposed by four members are immediately admitted to the privileges of the Institution, and pay on election ten guineas (five guineas as an admission fee and five guineas as the first annual payment). This payment secures admission to all lectures delivered in the Institution, to the libraries, and to the weekly evening meetings, with certain other privileges—such as the right of admitting two friends to the Friday evening meetings—a privilege often abused on occasions when a lion of unusual magnitude is about to roar. An inferior kind of member is the annual subscriber, who enjoys most of the privileges above named, with the exception of admission to the weekly meetings, from which sublime gatherings he is excluded. Other persons are suffered to subscribe to the afternoon lectures at the very moderate price of two guineas for all courses of lectures from Christmas to Midsummer, but are not allowed to show themselves elsewhere than in the lecture theatre, and never there on a Friday night.

This weekly meeting is a wonderful combination of science and society, of physics and fashion, albeit once in a while a printer or photographer manages to obtain permission to dilate on the excellence of his wares, and to thus advertise himself. Nevertheless, in spite of an occasional drawback of this kind, the Friday evening lectures are of sufficiently high class to please all but a purely scientific audience. It is clear that to gratify the members—who are, after all, mere flesh and blood, and not philosophical abstractions—concessions to popular taste and feeling must occasionally be made. Thus, while all may equally enjoy a lecture on the Acoustic Transparency and Opacity of the Atmosphere—a subject which, in its practical relation to fog-signals, is full of general interest—those of a higher and drier turn of mind experience ineffable delight when Professor Sylvester holds forth on the conversion of circular into parallel motion; while the noble army of simple lion-hunters rush not only to hear, but to see, Sir Samuel Baker. On this particular night I find all the approaches to Albemarle Street blocked by carriages, and on making my way into the Royal Institution find the theatre fully occupied at a quarter-past eight o'clock, or three quarters of an hour before the time of the lecture. With the exception of a few seats reserved for the two boards of Managers and Visitors, the hall is crowded to the ceiling, every avenue being already jammed with a dense mass of people, among whom gay opera cloaks and *Angot* caps largely predominate over black coats and snowy shirt-fronts. A few young men are visible, but after standing about for a while and finding it impossible to approach their far friend, these youths vanish through the crowded doorway and are seen no more, thus leaving the entire field clear to the British matron, who prevails to-night to an extent that would have struck terror into the soul of poor Nathaniel Hawthorne. There is no inconsiderable amount of crowding and pushing in this elegant throng, and I am forcibly reminded of the saying of a certain philosopher—who has seen men and cities, and the customs of them—that "a well-dressed crowd is a rude crowd."

So thoroughly and completely packed is every bench, step, and doorway, that it occurs to me as a piece of singular luck that no formidable philosophic apparatus is necessary for a dissertation on the Slave Trade of the White Nile, as the space often occupied by Professor Tyndall's tubs is packed full of chairs, to the great relief of a number of ladies. Sir Samuel Baker delivers his views on the Slave Trade to an evidently sympathetic audience, easily put into good humour by being told that England was the first nation to set the world the noble example of liberating her slaves—a statement, by the way, not precisely accurate, inasmuch as in 1780 was passed an Act for the gradual extinction of slavery in Pennsylvania, an example followed four years later by the States of New Jersey and Connecticut, and in 1793 the French abolished slavery in Hayti, forty years before its abolition in our West Indian Colonies. No doubt to those who had never heard much about slavery the remarks on its cruelty and injustice were interesting enough, but I, *infelix*, have had my ears too often pierced by shrill American voices, raised to shrieking pitch on this subject, during "the late trouble." Sir Samuel Baker is an excellent advocate for a new crusade against slavery, and produces ample evidence as to the atmosphere of general rascality evolved by slave-holding and slave-dealing, but his arguments, though true enough, are not very new. The lecturer, however, possesses the excellent gift of carrying his audience along with him, and sends them home happy in the conviction that they have assisted at an anti-slavery demonstration.

The claims of science are amply vindicated on the following Friday by Dr. Wright, an experimentalist of known boldness, who delivers a discourse on the "Chemical Changes Accompanying the Smelting of Iron in the Blast-Furnace." Dr. Wright has enjoyed the advantage of pursuing his investigations in concert with Mr. Lowthian Bell, a gentleman well known by his inquiries into the chemistry of the blast-furnace, as well as by his office as President of the Iron and Steel Institute, and his gigantic enterprises in the production of iron and chemicals. Although of little interest to the general public, this lecture commands a good attendance of experts, who follow Dr. Wright very attentively through his exposition, and endure, without a murmur, an atmosphere heavily charged with noxious gases.

I have already observed that, in addition to the Friday evening meetings, where lions of the first magnitude roar by turns, several courses of afternoon lectures, in which actual teaching is combined with attractive experiments, are given during the session. These lecturers and their subjects attract audiences of varying strength. Looking in, one afternoon, to hear a lecture on Palæontology by Professor Duncan, I find the theatre but thinly attended, in spite of the interesting character of the lecture and its eloquent treatment by the expositor. This apathy may perhaps be explained by the difficulty of inspiring ordinary human beings with a taste for science, pure and simple; as I well recollect that when—at the dawn of the Darwinian system—palæontological lectures were unavoidably associated with the controversy initiated by that philosopher, every lecture directly or indirectly bearing on the theory of Development commanded a numerous and fashionable audience. Attentive listeners sought, in the discourses of Professor Owen, for facts and deductions more or less damaging to the bold theory advanced in the now famous "Origin of Species by Natural Selection." But the uproar occasioned by the "Essays and Reviews," and Mr. Frederic Harrison's review of the reviewers in the "Westminster," has nearly subsided, and the polemical element has faded out of geological discussion. Denuded of its controversial spice, palæontology no longer possesses its whilom attractiveness, and the audience of to-day is apparently composed of those who care for the subject for its own sake alone. Professor Duncan is discoursing on that friend of my youth, the *ichthyosaurus*, and in a few neat and graphic sentences describes the manners, customs, and peculiar structure of the great fish-lizard, with whale-like body, crocodile head, and monstrous saucer-eyes. The *plesiosaur* with the outline described by the late Professor Buckland as that of a "turtle with a serpent pulled through it" next engages attention, and is described very graphically as a "longshore-man" of the diluvial period, a prowler on the edges of the great deep, and a snapper-up of unconsidered trifles. *Plesiosaurus* disposed of, the inevitable *pterodactyle* turns up, the flying lizard of predatory habits, the possible progenitor of birds, and the certain original of the heraldic dragon and griffin. The shape of the head and the gradual adoption by this gruesome creature of a breast-bone give still more coherence to the theory that *pterodactyle* is a lizard which is rapidly making up his mind to become a bird. These particulars, and a dissertation on coral islands, make up the body of an interesting lecture, which fails, however, to warm the audience into enthusiasm. Perhaps people don't care for coral islands, or mayhap, to parody a line of Mr. Bret Harte—"the *pterodactyle's* played out."

On another raw afternoon, about three p.m., I betake myself to Albemarle Street, and become the spectator of a widely different scene. The theatre is already full of eager visitors and thirsters after science, when elucidated by those brilliant experiments which excite the admiration and envy of Professor Tyndall's imitators—I had almost written rivals, forgetting that in this country, and in his own particular line of physical demonstration, Dr. John Tyndall, F.R.S., philosopher and cragsman, has no rival. At a three o'clock lecture many ladies are, of course, present, in all the variety of gorgeous array at present in fashion, for however severe may be the mental attributes of these fair students of physical science, no sternness is ever visible in their outward appearance. Pending the arrival of the professor of natural philosophy, these young ladies are chatting pleasantly among themselves. Are they talking science, I wonder, or discussing the merits of the Leonardo da Vinci hat, or the grace and style communicated by the Norwegian waistbelt, with all sorts of turnip watches and other quaint odds and ends dangling from it? Do they know much about liquids and gases, or have they come to learn? Verily, I know not. The well-known lecture table is covered with apparatus, and a huge bath tub occupies a considerable space. Mr. Cottrell, the laboratory assistant, is very busy, till, punctual to the stroke of three, a tall slender man, of undeniably Scottish aspect, steps to his place behind the lecture table, and a murmur of applause proclaims the satisfaction of the audience at the arrival of the successor of Faraday. The lecture, interesting in itself, is rendered doubly so by numerous and beautiful experiments, which succeed with infallible certainty. Perhaps the listeners to Professor Tyndall are accustomed to see his experiments "come off" in this way, but the traveller in search of science often sees experiments—chemical, physical, and others—break down with provoking perversity. No approach to anything like failure occurs to-day, and the applause is great on the light-carrying power of water being demonstrated by an experiment of singular beauty. The prescribed hour appears unnaturally short when the clock strikes, the lecture is closed by a short sentence, and, amid a mighty rustling of silks, the audience prepares to depart. For a few minutes a talkative crowd blocks up the wide staircase and hall, and a sort of scramble takes place for the carriages of which Albemarle Street is full. Fashion takes its departure, and, having laid in science enough to last for a week, leaves the professor to enjoy himself in his admirably-appointed laboratory.

As I wend my way homewards I reflect on the large amount of good solid work that has been done in the laboratories of the Royal Institution during the last seventy years, and on the effect produced by the dissemination of scientific knowledge among the upper classes. As a firm believer in the doctrine that all revolutions in taste must take their inception above and gradually percolate through the several strata of society, I keenly sympathize with the efforts of the Royal Institution towards inoculating the *grand monde* with a love for scientific investigation. Following the example of the sun—which first illumines the mountain tops, and later in the day penetrates into the deeper valleys—knowledge, striking first on the upper social regions, gradually descends, until all sorts and conditions of men are irradiated by its peaceful light.

III.

THE SOCIETY OF ARTS.

Like its younger sister in Albemarle Street, the Society of Arts is a notable instance of that drifting faculty which exercises so great an influence on all human institutions. Launched with widely-differing objects on the stream of events, these societies have in a certain measure displaced each other. The Royal Institution, now devoted to literature, and in a greater degree to pure science, was originally founded to promote those objects which have been fostered by the elder society, which, drifting away from Art in its highest sense, has taken in hand industrial art, and applied science. One single comparison will demonstrate my meaning. In the beginning of the century —under the auspices of Count Rumford—the Royal Institution undertook to improve the dwellings of the working classes, to warm and ventilate workhouses, hospitals, and cottages, and to exhibit and patronize improvements in the economical consumption of fuel and the teaching of culinary science. In the present year the Society of Arts, founded originally to encourage young artists, has offered premiums for the best kinds of culinary and domestic warming apparatus, and has directly fostered attempts to instruct the people of England in the best methods of preparing food.

The Society of Arts has now existed for a hundred and twenty years, and owes its foundation to Mr. William Shipley, a landscape painter, who, from a "well-grounded persuasion of the extensive utility of the art of drawing to this nation, erected the Academy in the Strand, opposite to Exeter Change." By the efforts of this gentleman a meeting was held in 1754 at Rawthmell's coffee-house, to consider the propriety of establishing a Society for the Encouragement of Arts, Manufactures, and Commerce.

It was resolved to bestow premiums on a certain number of boys and girls, and an advertisement was issued accordingly. The industrial element, however, was not lost sight of, as while a number of drawing prizes were advertised, premiums were offered for the discovery of cobalt in England, the growth of madder, and the manufacture of buff leather. The primary object was the encouragement of art, but the view taken of the "polite arts" was a sufficiently wide one, inasmuch as the premiums offered under this head were ultimately grouped under 196 classes. Many prizes were awarded for drawing, and among the recipients was Richard Cosway, who afterwards became a Royal Academician, and a portrait painter of repute. It was soon found necessary to confine the objects of study to certain models, and as no public museum or National Gallery then existed, individual collections, such as that formed by the Duke of Richmond, were selected for study.

On the consolidation of the Society the artists of London applied for permission to hold an exhibition in the Society's rooms. This permission was granted, and exhibitions continued to be held for several years. This annual inspection of the works of rival artists, who formed themselves into separate bodies, excited emulation, directed public attention towards their works, and ultimately secured for them the royal patronage and protection. These first exhibitions of pictures by native artists in the rooms of the Society of Arts may, therefore, be regarded as the origin of that exhibition of the Royal Academy which now forms one of the great events of the London season.

While the encouragement of art—pure and simple —thus formed the main object of the Society, investigation was directed towards many practical subjects related to the central idea. Endeavours were made to improve the materials employed by artists, and much attention was devoted to the various engraving processes as they gradually came into vogue. Wood engraving, aquatint, and mezzotint, were the subject of anxious care, as were improvements in pigments, oils, and varnishes.

Bronze casting and chasing, iron castings, and artistic metal work, were also encouraged, and at a later date, when Alois Senefelder, an actor of Munich, discovered lithography, the new art was first introduced to this country under the auspices of the Society of Arts. Steel engraving was also first taken seriously in hand by Mr. Charles Warren, chairman of the Fine Arts Committee, who, at the suggestion of Mr. Gill, chairman of the Mechanics Committee, adopted a new method of treating steel plates. Previously to this, many attempts had been made to engrave on steel. Albert Dürer is said to have etched on steel, and there are four plates etched by this artist, impressions of which exist in the British Museum, and which in all books of art are recorded as having been executed on steel. In the attempts to revive this art, pieces of saw-blades were selected as the most promising material, but these efforts were attended with very little success. A Mr. Raimbach then endeavoured to engrave on blocks of steel, but without achieving any material advance. Mr. Gill now drew the attention of Mr. Warren to the method employed at Birmingham in the manufacture of ornamental snuffers and other articles of cast steel. The process employed at Birmingham was "to subject the steel, after having been rolled into sheets, to the process of decarbonization, by means of which it is converted to a very pure soft iron, being then made into the required instrument or other article. The ornamental work is engraved or impressed on the soft metallic surface, which, by cementation with proper materials, is again converted superficially into steel. Mr. Warren modified this process, and obtained thin plates of steel capable of being acted upon by acids and cut with the graver, without destroying the cutting edge of the tool—as was the case with the saw-blades. The resulting plate yielded a greatly increased number of impressions." When brought to perfection, steel plates were found equal to the production of ten or twelve times the number of impressions yielded by copper plates. Capital was invested in the production of works of a high class, with the effect of spreading far and wide through the country myriads of prints calculated to elevate and improve the taste of the people. This process of conversion and reconversion of steel was soon afterwards applied by Perkins to the production of steel rollers. These were first softened and then pressed into the engraved surface of a hardened steel block, and having acquired a design in relief were themselves hardened in their turn, and by being applied to softened steel plates produced almost indefinite multiplication of the original engraved plate. For commercial purposes this invention proved of immense value in the production of bank notes, receipts, and postage stamps.

To ignore the exertions of the Society of Arts in the direction of agriculture, and especially arboriculture, would be to omit an important page in its history. The introduction of new varieties of grasses and roots was sedulously encouraged, while drill ploughs, the drainage of land, root slicers, chaff cutters, scarifiers, reaping machines, threshing machines, and means of harvesting hay and corn in wet seasons, were all subjects of premiums. Big things and little things came in for their share of attention. In the early days of the Society sheep were marked with tar, to the great loss of wool-growers. The Society sought strenuously to modify and improve the mode of marking sheep, and meanwhile instituted a crusade against that bold invader, the Norway rat, who had recently overrun the country.

The preservation of timber was an object of earnest solicitude. In this age, when coal has effectually displaced wood as a heat producer, and iron has been successfully applied to the construction of houses and ships, it is difficult to realize the anxiety of our forefathers at seeing whole forests destroyed for smelting purposes. For a long time past the work of destruction had been going on, when the Society of Arts stepped in to advocate the planting of trees on a large scale. The production of oak was a special object of the Society's attention, the planting of acorns was carried on to a very large extent, and gold medals for raising that description of timber were awarded to many noblemen and gentlemen, among whom were the Earl of Wilton, the Marquis of Tichfield, Mr. Morse, Mr. Curwen, and others. The cultivation of the ash—for which the Bishop of Llandaff received a gold medal—of the Scotch fir and larch, and of fruit trees generally, received active encouragement. Under the auspices of the Society millions of trees were planted, to the enrichment and adornment of many previously barren slopes. It is worthy of remark that to a neglect of these precautions is assigned an actual change of the climatic conditions of parts of Italy, and that the reduction of the Arno to an insignificant stream is ascribed to the reckless denudation of the mountains among which that historic river takes its rise. Travellers in Switzerland also have not failed to observe in the side valleys many relics of ancient mines, deserted, at last, because all the wood within carrying distance had been recklessly destroyed without any attempt being made to replace it by planting.

Considerable effort was devoted to encouraging the introduction and culture of spices into the British possessions. The cinnamon tree was introduced into Jamaica ; the nutmeg plant into St. Vincent; the clove tree into Trinidad; the mango and the bread-fruit tree were also planted in the West Indies. Attention was also directed towards such imports as were capable of discovery, manufacture, and culture at home.

Cobalt was discovered in Cornwall; buff leather and its manufacture improved ; copper and brass vessels were tinned ; and hemp, flax, and madder were cultivated for the use of our manufacturers. "Saw-mills were built; our fish supply improved; and the curing of fish encouraged. Upon the fish trade alone the Society expended many thousands of pounds, and succeeded in establishing a regular supply to the London markets."

During the greater part of its career the Society thus addressed itself to the task of fostering the useful arts. One condition, however, was, in the early days of the Society, rigidly insisted upon. The inventor who sought to obtain recognition of his discovery was obliged to forego the idea of patenting his work. What was given to the world by the assistance of the Society of Arts, was to be given freely and openly for the benefit of all. Although this principle would find many and eloquent advocates at the present day, a period intervened during which it was found necessary to make concessions to patentees. The introduction of steam as a motive power led to a sudden and immense development of mechanical ingenuity, and swelled the prospective reward of a successful inventor to such large proportions that it was no longer probable that men would work for honour and glory alone. Eventually patentees were permitted to read papers before the Society of Arts, which, during the greater part of a century, continued to take an active interest in advancing the interests of science, and in affording aid and countenance to the other societies of less catholic tendencies, which sprang rapidly into existence. As has been already pointed out, the Royal Academy in its youth owed much to the Society of Arts; and it is worthy of note that, not only was the first exhibition of the works of rival artists held in the Society's rooms, but the first collection of photographs exhibited there in 1853. The Society still maintains a liberal tone, and is generous enough to grant the use of its handsome room to many societies for the purpose of holding their various meetings.

If the Society in the Adelphi merit a place of honour as a promoter of other societies, still more does it demand notice as the mother of exhibitions. Its exhibitional maternity was shown in this wise. In the year 1841 the Society of Arts, like many other originally active bodies, had shown signs of falling into decrepitude. For many of the purposes for which it was originally established its office had been filled by other institutions, which, being less expansive in their views, appeared likely to act towards the mother society like young ducks hatched by a barn-door hen, and take to the stream of the future without consulting the feelings of their foster-parent. The Society was obviously falling into the sere and yellow leaf, and it was clear that something had to be done to rejuvenate it. A committee was appointed to revise the working of the Society, and that body recommended that a Council to manage the affairs of the Society should be instituted. The committee in its report also gave expression to the conviction "that the Society cannot continue to exist on the plan of proceeding which is at present pursued," and that "the object of the Society is the promotion of the useful arts rather than the personal gratification of the members." It was further recommended that six commitees should be established, of five members each, and many other valuable pieces of advice were tendered, but nothing came of all this for the time being. At length, however, measures were taken for obtaining a Royal Charter of Incorporation, finally granted in 1847, and in the mean time it was proposed that an Exhibition of English Industry, analogous to those held abroad, should be instituted. The first action taken in this direction was an offer of special prizes for articles of manufacture, and a special fund was obtained for this purpose by private subscription. It was deemed necessary to stimulate the makers of English pottery to efforts towards an artistic combination of form and colour. A committee of artists was appointed to adjudge the prize for a tea-service, and this was awarded to a set designed by "Felix Summerly," and manufactured by Messrs. Minton. The identity of "Felix Summerly" was then disclosed, and the Society's silver medal was presented to Mr. Henry Cole (who has since received the Companionship of the Bath), on the 12th of June, 1846. From this date a notable change came over the constitution of the Society. Yearly exhibitions were held. It is true that these were of a sectional character, and only proposed to illustrate certain branches of English industry; but it is not the less true that they were the immediate precursors of the Great Exhibition of 1851. Prizes for modern industrial art were offered, and were eagerly competed for. Manufactures and artistic productions were got together at great expenditure of cash and industry, with the effect of rapidly increasing the number of members. In 1847, the members of the Society numbered scarce five hundred; but within three years these numbers had tripled. But, in 1849, there were "croakers" in the camp. Not a few of the ruling spirits were inclined to "look back from the plough." As an instance of this may be quoted a recommendation of the Finance Committee of 1849, that "the exhibitions be discontinued," and another, passed in December of the same year, that "it is expedient to reconsider the policy of an Art Manufacture Exhibition in the year 1850." But the advanced spirits of the Society were not to be baulked. Against the council of the ancients a formidable opposition was organized. Mr. Cole resigned his seat on the Council, and, biding his time till the general meeting, effected a noteworthy *coup d'état*. On election day the reactionary party were ousted by an immense majority, and an entirely new Council elected. The Exhibition of Ancient and Mediæval Art was duly held, and resulted in a splendid success, and a complete revolution of the financial condition of the association. In 1850 the debts of the Society amounted to £2402, an amount that was reduced in 1851 to £1696, since when the Society has become not only solvent, but possessed of a large accumulation of capital, which—in the opinion of many of the members, now amounting to over 3000—

it is somewhat chary in dispensing. This great storm, which completely altered the condition of the Society of Arts, and culminated in the Great Exhibition of 1851, can thus be distinctly traced to Mr. Felix Summerly's "tea-cup."

The merit of initiating the idea of an International Exhibition has been often warmly contested, but there is no longer any doubt that the original proposition was made to the Committee of the Society of Arts in 1844, by Sir William Fothergill Cooke. There is no question that the idea of this gentleman was clearly that of an International Exhibition, at that time declined by the Committee of the Society of Arts, but at a later period adopted by that body with the sanction and co-operation of the late Prince Consort.

In the month of June, 1849, the secretary, Mr. J. Scott Russell, stated at the annual meeting, in the presence of the late Prince Consort, that, owing to the yearly increasing success of the Society's Exhibition, the Council had no doubt of their being able to carry out the plan originally proposed for holding a great national exhibition of the products of British industry in 1851. This statement led to frequent communications between His Royal Highness the president, and various members, with the ultimate result of expanding the plan to international dimensions. The Prince Consort, as president of the Society, brought the scheme officially under the notice of the Government; but in the mean while the Society of Arts was not idle, and had already entered into a contract for building a convenient edifice, when a royal commission was issued. Mr. Scott Russell and Mr.—now Sir—Stafford Northcote were appointed secretaries. An executive committee was formed, consisting of "Henry Cole, Charles Wentworth Dilke the younger, George Drew, Francis Fuller, and Robert Stephenson, with Matthew Digby Wyatt as secretary." Meanwhile the Society of Arts had organized the financial arrangements necessary for carrying out the scheme, but the immediate connection of the Society with the Exhibition now came to an end; the child had outgrown its nurse, and required nothing short of a royal commission to manage it. How well the Exhibition of 1851 was managed, and how after the final adjustment of accounts a surplus of £186,438 18*s*. 6*d*. remained in hand, are now matters of history, as well as the expenditure of that sum as part of the money devoted to the purchase and development of the Gore House estate.

Since the launching of the Great Exhibition, the Society of Arts has done much good work in promoting industrial art and encouraging inventive genius. It is true that much of its work has been taken out of its hands by the societies and museums to which it has given rise. Among these is the Photographic Society, whose inception was due to the exhibition organized by Dr. Diamond. The South Kensington Museum itself may be fairly regarded as an offshoot of the Mediæval Exhibition, while the Government Department of Science and Art is directly descended from the parent body. But the mission of the Society is not to repose on its laurels. It comes to the fore with a formidable list of premiums, at the head of which is a series of gold medals and prizes of £50 for improved cooking and warming apparatus; £500 are devoted to this purpose, and have been placed at the disposal of the Society by a single member. A large number of prizes in money, and many gold and silver medals, are also offered to inventors. Much interest is excited at the present moment concerning the award of the Albert Gold Medal, a prize established in memory of the late Prince Consort, to reward "distinguished merit in promoting arts, manufactures, or commerce." This medal was first presented in 1864 to Sir Rowland Hill, K.C.B., in 1865 to the late Emperor of the French, and in 1866 to Faraday. Since then, this distinguishing mark of the Society's appreciation has been conferred on Wheatstone, Whitworth, Liebig, Henry Cole, Henry Bessemer, and has this year been awarded by the council to Dr. C. W. Siemens, "for his researches in connection with the laws of heat, and the practical applications of them to furnaces used in the arts; and for his improvements in the manufacture of iron; and generally for the services rendered by him in connection with economization of fuel in its various applications to manufactures and the arts."

For some years the Society's examinations, conducted through local institutions about the country, have assisted the spread of general education, and now that this work is being more completely executed by the University local examinations, the Society has set on foot a scheme of technological examinations, which it is hoped may bear good fruit.

The members of the Society are supplied with ample entertainment by the ordinary meetings, the lectures endowed by Dr. Cantor, and the meetings of the African, Indian, and chemical sections. For the very moderate sum of two guineas per annum they are allowed to attend meetings, to introduce two visitors, and moreover to receive a copy of the weekly journal published by the Society. Prior to 1852, no *Journal of the Society of Arts* existed, the Society being content with a somewhat meagre volume of Transactions. With the new era of prosperity the *Journal* was happily inaugurated, and now supplies members of the Society with a complete record of the weekly proceedings, together with such admixture of general scientific or technical matter as may be deemed necessary by the editor, Mr. H. T. Wood. With the growth of the Society its organ has, of course, increased in importance, and during the last year or two, especially, has been considerably improved. Not the least valuable part of the *Journal* is the preservation of the discussions which generally ensue on the reading of a paper, and occasionally exceed in importance the paper itself.

In the course of my travels I have had many opportunities of enjoying the discussions at John Street, Adelphi. Just before entering the spacious and handsome "great room," adorned by Barry's well-known pictures, I find a notice that any gentleman wishing to take part in the discussion should make his name known to the secretary, Mr. P. Le Neve Foster. This notice has always appeared to me as a sort of "fiery cross," or summons to immediate action, calling upon me then and there to "pull myself together," collect my scattered wits, and hold myself in readiness to jump up at the right moment and contradict everybody. As a rule, I succeed in crushing this feeling, and follow my general plan of retiring into myself, and waiting until called for; but there are moments when my amazement at finding that I understand the subject overcomes my natural timidity, and I say, "Ha! ha!" among the captains.

Inasmuch as the ordinary meetings are understood

to be held for the express purpose of ventilating new ideas or pet crotchets, it is only natural to suppose that the fun of these meetings exists in the discussion. To those of an unregenerate nature there is always something objectionable in being talked to, or talked at, without a chance of reply. There is no man whom I love and revere more than my friend the Rev. Mr. Chasuble. He is a good classic and a good fellow, generous and hearty, a good logician, and a worthy gentleman, whom I love everywhere but in the pulpit, where he has it all his own way. I admire Professor Stillmore immensely, and love to hear him discourse excellent science, except on those occasions when he appears behind the lecture-table as another and very inferior being to the real Stillmore, whom I delight to cultivate. Holding these heathenish views, and loving not to sit at the feet of any Gamaliel whatsoever, I enjoy myself hugely at the Society of Arts. I know that, so soon as the lecture is announced, somebody will make up his mind to come down and contradict all the statements advanced. No sooner does the victim appear at the reading-desk than I glance round the room, and often succeed in detecting those who come to argue—if not "to scoff." These critics know all about the subject, whether it be Frozen Beef or a Channel Tunnel. They become feverish if the reader of the paper be slow or at all inarticulate, and they look keenly at his diagrams, meaning to make short work of those productions in due season. For his allotted space the reader is suffered to proceed without let or hindrance; but no sooner has he made an end of his reading, than well-informed gentlemen—who have either been listening attentively or, as is more probable, been thinking over what they should say when he had done—spring up and proceed to demolish him bit by bit. After a while, a reaction sets in, the friends of the lecturer support him more or less warmly — generally less — and the battle becomes general all along the line. The hero of the evening has the right of reply, so that the much-valued privilege of the last word rests with him.

Under these regulations, there is often much healthy talk, and occasionally some good "tossing and goring"—a quotation which reminds me that its author was one of the early debaters of the Adelphi, and that a "subject relating to mechanics" was once descanted upon at the Society of Arts and Manufactures, with a "propriety, perspicuity, and energy which excited general admiration," by no less a personage than Dr. Samuel Johnson.

IV.

THE INSTITUTION OF CIVIL ENGINEERS.

Whatever diverse opinions may be held as to the stationary or progressive nature of the moral sciences, and although art may be said to have actually retrograded since the age of Pericles, no doubt can exist as to the enormous advance in wealth and comfort made by the civilized world during this present century—emphatically the century of the straight line. It is probable that an ancient Athenian gentleman was at least as well instructed in metaphysical science as a modern graduate of Oxford or Edinburgh, Heidelberg or Halle. So far as keen artistic sense and purity of taste are concerned, the Greek—with eye educated by the constant contemplation of forms of perfect beauty—with ear attuned to the sounding march of Homer's hexameters, and with mind accustomed to dwell on the stern grandeur of Æschylus, the polished lines of Sophocles, and the more sympathetic verse of Euripides—possessed an unquestionable advantage over the modern scholar, whose attentive perusal of novels and newspapers is hardly calculated to improve his oratory. If, however, it may be conceded that no advance has been made—nay, more, that actual retrogression has taken place—during the last 2500 years in the study of words and their uses, and in the production of beautiful forms, it must, on the other hand, be admitted that the modern Englishman possesses a knowledge of *things* and wields a power over the forces of nature undreamt of by the poets, philosophers, and grammarians who discoursed sweetly in the garden, or thundered out sonorous periods in the Agora. Most worthy of note is the marvellously short space of time in which the great modern development of human power has taken place. Albeit a hardy plant, science has grown with almost inconceivable rapidity. In some five or six thousand years man had only improved the canoe and the coracle into a galley and a sailing ship, and had shown even less inventive genius in the methods of terrestrial locomotion—indeed, so far as roads were concerned, England was worse off 200 years ago than during the period of the Roman occupation. Something had been done in widening the minds of men by making them better acquainted with the globe that they inhabited. Vasco de Gama and Columbus had unlocked the treasures of the Eastern and Western World; the mariners' compass had come into general use; Copernicus, Tycho Brahé, and Galileo had made short work of traditional cosmogonies, and those potent civilizers, the printing-press and gunpowder, had been invented. But the material condition of mankind had as yet received no immediate benefit from these discoveries. The wealth of Mexico and Peru, far from enriching Spain, had diverted from the parent country the energy of her bravest sons, and the loss of the Low Countries had inflicted on the State a loss from which she has never since recovered. France was occupied in the pursuit of glory; Holland, rich and prosperous beyond all European nations, was harassed with the task of Joshua—in staying the sun of Louis Quatorze; while England had as yet given but small promise of the industrial pre-eminence she was destined ultimately to assume. Nevertheless indications were not wanting in our little island of a strong desire for material progess, due, according to some authorities, to the great awakening of the human mind during the period of the Renaissance, and according to others to the inductive system of philosophy propounded by Bacon. Be this as it may, an inquiring spirit was abroad, and investigations into the then hidden forces of nature—with the direct intention of pressing them into the service of mankind

—occupied the minds of many eminent Englishmen. Robert Boyle rendered important services to science, and hovered on the brink of other yet more important discoveries. Newton, Flamsteed, and Halley immortalized themselves by their contributions to astronomy; but most remarkable of all were the sudden strides made in the arts of construction, in which the celebrated Hooke greatly distinguished himself. Leuwenhoeck raised the microscope to the dignity of a scientific instrument, under Savery the first crude steam-engine was brought into working order and employed as an efficient agent for raising water, and Newton invented the reflecting telescope. So far as the sudden advance in mechanical science which signalized the last century can be assigned to any one person it may be ascribed to this great man, whose "Principia" revealed the method of applying mathematical principles to the forces of nature.

All this admirable seed, destined to bear fruit an hundred and a thousand fold in due season, did not of course produce any immediate amelioration in the condition of the British nation. More than any other nation England might, as late as a hundred and fifty years ago, have been pronounced singularly deficient in public works. While Holland—and for that matter India and China—possessed a vast system of canals, the internal communications of this country were in a barbarous condition. Artificial harbours, canals, and machinery there were none, and the public roads across the country were for the most part little better than bridle paths. Over these primitive and deeply-rutted tracks, often impassable in wet weather, the few wheeled carriages in use were dragged, at a fearful expenditure of sinew, time, and temper. A county magnate, on the occasion of one of his rare visits to London, set his affairs in order before starting, and packing a lumbering coach with ample provision, trusted to the strength of six or eight powerful Flanders horses to drag him through the tedious miles of mire which separated him from the metropolis, holding himself fortunate indeed if he escaped breaking down more than half-a-dozen times on the road, and eluded the attentions of professional or amateur highwaymen. So long as the roads remained mere muddy tracks it was found convenient to avoid as much as possible the use of wheeled carriages. The "solitary horseman" and the "two travellers," beloved of romancists, picked their way among the stones and quagmires which separated one great town from another, and the commerce of the country was mainly carried on by means of pack-horses.

Owing to the difficulty and danger of transit, the luxuries of life were exorbitantly dear, and even those necessaries which did not happen to grow in the immediate vicinity of the consumer were difficult of attainment. In the total absence of canals, inland navigation was both tedious and uncertain. "The rivers were left," as the Eastern potentate remarked, "as Allah had made them;" and therefore this imperfect river navigation could only be undertaken under favourable circumstances, *i.e.* when the rivers were sufficiently flooded. In a few rare instances temporary flush-weirs were used to pen up the water in shallow places, and in a few others side cuts with the pound lock were introduced, with side weirs constructed with the double object of allowing the floods to escape and utilizing the water-power.

During the first quarter of the last century Newcomen's steam-engine, having been improved by Potter and Beighton so as to become self-acting, was used for pumping water from collieries, but the consumption of fuel was so great that its application continued to be very limited. For driving such machinery as existed, and for working the few mills in operation, wind and water were the sole motive powers employed, and with the exception of the silk mills at Derby, introduced by Sir Thomas Lombe from Italy, nothing in the shape of manufacturing machinery was known. Metallurgy was yet in its infancy—charcoal being the chief medium used for reducing iron—sanitary precautions were unknown—

the magnificent *cloaca* of Rome having found no mediæval successors—paving was neglected, and gas as yet undreamt of.

A great change was at hand. A revolution in the face of England was about to be wrought by three remarkable men—the fathers of modern scientific engineering. In 1716 James Brindley was born at Chapel-en-le-Frith, in Derbyshire. Eight years later John Smeaton was born at Austhorpe, near Leeds; and in 1736 James Watt saw the light at Greenock. If strict definition be adhered to, Watt can hardly be classed as a civil engineer, although he proposed a plan for improving the river Clyde, and suggested the idea of the Caledonian Canal, before devoting himself exclusively to the improvement of the steam-engine, and working out those grand discoveries which have immortalized his name.

Although born later than Brindley, Smeaton was the first to distinguish himself—a circumstance attributable probably to the comparative ease of his circumstances, and from his having no educational leeway to make up in manhood. Commencing with a fair education, and devoting himself for a short space to the study of the law, Smeaton soon discovered that the bent of his genius was in another direction, and being luckily not thwarted by his parents, applied his vigorous mind to philosophical inquiry. Starting in life as a mathematical instrument maker in 1750, he two years later attracted the notice of the scientific world by his air-pump, and subsequently, by several communications to the Royal Society on mechanical subjects, so raised himself in the estimation of that learned body as to obtain their gold medal, and the honour of being elected a Fellow of the Society. The celebrated paper on the natural powers of wind and water to turn mills and other machinery depending on circular motion produced directly and indirectly the most important results. Owners of water-power discovered that their power was increased one-third by the adoption of Smeaton's plan. Subsequent improvements were made on Smeaton's system for windmills, which by Meikle, Bywater, and Cubitt were brought—as were high-roads and mail coaches—to absolute perfection just as they were about to be thrust from the world by steam.

Smeaton next devoted his attention to the laws which govern the formation and the maintenance of harbours, and, after inspecting the great works in operation in Holland, introduced many improvements in the draining of marsh lands. About the middle of the last century a perfect rage sprung up for public works, and, in the conduct of these, Smeaton never once failed. Curiously enough, his first important work is that with which he is most immediately identified. At the very period—1755-59—when he was unknown and untried as a practical engineer, he was selected as the fittest person to be entrusted with the rebuilding of the Eddystone Lighthouse, just destroyed by fire. By the design and construction of this celebrated edifice, Smeaton introduced a new era in masonry, and achieved one of the greatest triumphs that have ever fallen to the lot of an engineer.

While Smeaton was battling with the winds and waves, Brindley was struggling with the difficulties of emerging from an agricultural to a mechanical career. Born of humble—but as the American humourist hath it, "not otherwise dishonest"—parents, Brindley was, almost until manhood, entirely without education. Drifting afterwards into the millwright's trade, he acquired by his mechanical skill a certain provincial celebrity which, although not very lucrative in itself, yet paved the way to an engagement destined to immortalize Brindley and enrich his patron. Anterior to the career of Brindley, pound locks had been introduced on river navigations, and were also used on the Sankey Canal in 1755. This work was effected by making an almost entirely new channel, and its success gave a remarkable impetus to canal construction. In 1758 Brindley was called upon by the Duke of Bridgewater to advise on his project of a canal from Worsley to Manchester. Without unnecessary pondering or hesitation, Brindley forsook tradition, and, striking into a new path, placed the inland navigation of England far in advance of what had been achieved elsewhere.

He constructed—in addition to the Bridgewater Canal, with its many miles of underground communications in the Worsley coal mines, and its famous aqueduct at Barton — the celebrated Grand Trunk navigation, cutting through the mountainous backbone of England by the Harecastle tunnel. In conjunction with Smeaton and others he established water communication between the distant and apparently naturally divided towns of London, Liverpool, Bristol, and Hull, and justly acquired the title of father of inland navigation.

While Brindley and Smeaton were engaged in the construction of great public works, James Watt was giving up the best years of his life to the improvement of the steam-engine. Stated briefly, the inventions of Watt, which had the effect of bringing the steam-engine into general use, were as follows: the separate condensing vessel, with an air-pump for exhausting the steam cylinder, instead of injecting cold water into it for impelling the piston on Newcomen's plan by atmospheric pressure. In conjunction with Boulton, Watt brought these improvements into operation about the year 1773, and produced a greater diminution in the consumption of fuel than Smeaton, who had rendered the system of Newcomen as perfect as it could be made, had already done. The labour of the eight succeeding years resulted in the invention of rotatory motion by the steam-engine, first by the crank, and afterwards by the sun and planet wheel, thus adapting it to the driving of all kinds of machinery. A year later, Watt invented the application of steam with expansion and with double action, alternately above and below the piston, and in 1784 invented the parallel motion, or working gear and valves and the governor. These improvements being carried into effect in the engines made by Boulton and Watt in 1784-85 induced their introduction to mills, whence they have succeeded in expelling simpler applications of natural forces.

Concurrently with the advance made in the construction of harbours, lighthouses, canals, drainage works, and the steam-engine, great improvements were effected in the roads of the country. Food for melancholy reflection is supplied by the fact that many of the most important roads in the world have been made for purely military purposes—*i.e.*, to bear soldiers to kill people, not corn to feed them. The ancient Roman roads—admirably constructed as they were—owed their construction to strategic purposes, and the famous road over the Simplon was made with no other object but to facilitate the pouring of a French army into the plains of Lombardy. For like reasons a certain impetus was given to road-making in England by the raids of the two Pretenders; and by the direction of General Wade the first really good roads seen in this island since the decadence of the Romans were formed through the north of England into the Highlands. These works, constructed by military engineers, drew strong attention to the wretched condition of the ordinary roads of the country, which, as has been previously remarked, were simply worn tracks and nothing more. It is true that public or hackney coaches were established in London in 1625, but it was not until 1666 that a coach was established which travelled between London and Oxford in two days. Another, called the "Flying Coach," was afterwards started to perform the journey in thirteen successive hours—or at the rate of four miles an hour—but this unprecedented feat could only be accomplished during the summer months. In 1712 London and Edinburgh were connected by a service of coaches, but this journey occupied thirteen days, exactly the period required by the *Great Western* to perform her first voyage from Bristol to New York. Improvements in the construction of roads and of coaches were gradually introduced, and in 1784 passengers and letters were conveyed from London to Edinburgh in three days and nights, an achievement which created the most extraordinary excitement. This period was next reduced to forty-two hours, when the ultimate effect of animal spirit and endurance was reached. The transport of goods was enormously expensive and tedious. It required from two to three days to convey a ton of merchandise from Liverpool to Manchester, at a cost of forty shillings per ton, a service now performed in two or three hours for as many shillings.

In the construction of the improved high-roads which covered this island during the early part of the present century, a prominent part was taken by Thomas Telford, who, in conjunction with William Jessop and John Rennie, composed a trio of eminent engineers — the connecting link between the fathers of the craft and the generation of workers who, in our own day, have covered the globe with evidences of their skill. The labours of Jessop—the pupil, and afterwards the assistant, of Smeaton—reflected no discredit on his great teacher. Among the many great undertakings that he conducted to a successful conclusion may be mentioned the improvements on the rivers Aire, Calder, and Trent, the Grand Junction Canal, the inland navigation of

Ireland, the City ship-canal across the Isle of Dogs, and the conversion of that part of the river Avon which flows through the city of Bristol into an immense floating dock. Jessop was, moreover, the consulting engineer of the West India Dock Company in London, and of the Ellismere Canal Company. He also laid down the Surrey iron rail, or tramway, which, albeit a failure as a speculation, is worthy of note in a sketch of the progress of civil engineering as one of the earliest applications of this mode of conveyance to the purposes of public traffic.

John Rennie — whose name looms large in the annals of engineering — enjoyed the advantage of early training under the ingenious Meikle, the inventor of the threshing machine, and worked as an occasional student under some of the most celebrated professors of the University of Edinburgh. Commencing business as a millwright, in his native county of Haddingtonshire, he was soon led to change the scene of his labours in consequence of an introduction to James Watt, who invited him to superintend the erection of the Albion flour-mills, where the perfected machinery of Boulton and Watt was to be put into operation. Quickly acquiring reputation as a superior mechanist, he was appointed about the year 1791 or 1792 to direct the execution of the Lancaster Canal. This and the Crinan Canal, which divides the Mull of Cantire from Argyleshire, established his reputation as a civil engineer of the first rank. He was associated with other great works —the completion of the Eau Brink cut, and the new Nene outfall for the drainage of the fens of Norfolk, Lincoln, and Cambridgeshire. He also participated in the construction of three of the large dock establishments in the port of London, the Leith docks, and extensive additions to those of Liverpool and Hull. Still more stupendous operations now engaged his attention. Sheerness Dockyard was raised by him out of a quicksand 25 feet deep and 10 feet under low water. Pembroke was also designed by him, as were the breakwater in Plymouth Sound, the artificial harbours of Kingstown, Howth, Holyhead, and Donaghadee, together with three bridges over the Thames, and others in various parts of the country.

Thomas Telford—a Dumfriesshire man—enjoyed none of the advantages possessed by Rennie and Jessop, but advanced to a high position by the sheer force of that *perfervidum ingenium* with which the inhabitants of North Britain are supposed to be endowed. A native of Eskdale, he received the education commonly given to the peasantry of that country, and having been apprenticed to a stonemason, worked diligently at his trade until his twenty-third year. A visit to Edinburgh revealed to him a wider horizon than that of his native valley. Coming to London, and working for a time as a mason in the quadrangle of Somerset House—then building—he attracted attention by his superior intelligence, and was appointed to superintend the erection of a new official residence in Portsmouth Dockyard, and subsequently undertook the direction of some alterations in Shrewsbury Castle. In 1793 he was nominated acting engineer of the Ellesmere Canal. Albeit every part of England contains some record of Telford, his works were not confined to the United Kingdom; his skill was employed in the construction of the great ship-canal of Göta, in Sweden, the last connecting link in the navigation from the Baltic Sea to the German Ocean. The Caledonian Canal, originally proposed by Watt, and advised on by Jessop, was executed by Telford. Participating in the construction of many other great works—notably the Gloucester and Berkeley ship-canal—Telford is, perhaps, after all, best known by the gigantic system of roads executed under his superintendence—the Highland, the Holyhead, and the Glasgow and Carlisle, whereby "whole regions were brought within the pale of society." Besides the thousands of minor bridges forming part of these works, Telford constructed several bridges over the Severn, the Broomielaw bridge over the Clyde, the bridge over the Conway, and, lastly, the famous structure which spanned the Menai Straits. Telford closed a long and glorious career in 1834, and found a fitting tomb in Westminster Abbey, having lived to see the advent of the iron roads that were destined to consign to disuse many of the finest products of his genius.

The great development of civil engineering produced by the labours of himself and his contemporaries induced the illustrious Smeaton, so early as 1771, to found the society since known by his name. At that period the Royal Society absorbed nearly all those distinguished by scientific attainments. In the comparative infancy of scientific knowledge this was natural and possible from the very catholicity of that illustrious body, but as the objects of philosophical research multiplied, and the sphere of inquiry widened, many offshoots from the parent stem assumed an independent existence. The Royal Astronomical Society was the first of these, and was followed by associations for promoting the study of geology, botany, zoology, geography, and statistics. The Smeatonian Society of Civil Engineers had existed for nearly fifty years, when it was felt that the growing importance of civil engineering demanded an institution on a larger scale. Thomas Telford (himself a Smeatonian) concurred in this view, and an opportunity was soon found of carrying it into effect. Towards the end of 1817 a few gentlemen, then beginning life, resolved to form themselves into a society for promoting a regular intercourse between those engaged in the various branches of civil engineering, and "thereby mutually benefiting by the interchange of individual observation and experience." The first meeting was held at the King's Head Tavern, in Cheapside, on the 2nd January following, when rules were adopted for the government of the society, which continued to assemble for the next two years, when it was resolved "that a respectful communication be made to Thomas Telford, Esquire, civil engineer, to patronise the institution by taking upon himself the office of President." Telford accepted the chair without hesitation, and was formally installed on the 21st March following. Receiving a new impetus from this important accession of strength, the institution grew rapidly in importance, until on the 3rd of June, 1828, it received a charter of incorporation under the Great Seal by the title of the "Institution of Civil Engineers."

During the quarter of a century which elapsed between the formation of the Society and the occupation of the presidential chair by Sir John Rennie in 1846, the civil engineers of the United Kingdom had distinguished themselves not only at home, but in every quarter of the globe. Steam had asserted its empire on land and sea. Time and space had been reduced to their lowest terms. Projects for traversing water by boats worked by mechanical means appear to have occupied the attention of philosophers from remote periods—remote, that is, from an engineering point of view. The propulsion of boats by wheels is said to date as far back as the time of the Romans, and the Chinese are said to possess a boat moved by these means. Spain also puts in a claim on behalf of one Blasco de Garay, reported to have made an experiment in propelling vessels in the presence of the Emperor Charles V., at Barcelona, in 1543. Reverting to more exact history, we find Prince Rupert owning a barge propelled by wheels in 1682, when it was proposed to build tug-boats with wheels, worked by horses, for towing vessels against wind and tide; but the first idea of applying steam to the propulsion of ships appears to be due to the celebrated Papin, who in 1690 proposed to propel boats by racks and pinions, with pistons working in steam cylinders. This ingenious inventor had thought out this scheme very well, and was only deterred from putting it in practice by want of funds, a disease from which—at the period in question—the Royal Society, to whom Papin had applied, suffered severely,. In 1737, Jonathan Hulls published a pamphlet, wherein he gives a plate of a boat with a wheel attached to the stern, driven by a steam-engine to propel the boat—tugging behind her a vessel of war. He took out a patent for the invention, but experienced so much opposition that he relinquished the project. Newcomen's engine was proposed for propelling the wheel; but the difficulty of producing rotatory motion with that kind of engine explains the abandonment of the design. Nothing more was done until 1765, when Dr. Robison, of Edinburgh, proposed to James Watt to apply steam for propelling engines on land and sea. Watt, however, considered Newcomen's engine ill-calculated for this purpose, and devoted his entire energies to the perfection of his own form of engine, content to leave its manifold application to time.

In 1782 the Marquis de Jouffroi tried a steamboat on the Saône at Lyons, but without success. About the year 1788 Fitch and Ramsay, of America, and Serrati, an Italian, are said to have made some experiments, with what success is not known; and in the same year Miller, of Dalswinton, constructed a double boat, 60 feet long, with two paddle-wheels in the centre, moved by manual labour, and was convinced that power alone was wanting to bring his idea to full fruition. Taylor proposed to employ steam, and applied to Symington, a practical engineer (who had previously proposed some improvements in Newcomen's engine, with a view to propelling carriages), to supply him with an engine. This experiment was successful, so far as it went, and was followed by others; but the difficulty of avoiding an infringement of Watt's patent, and the trouble and annoyance occasioned by the opposition of mankind, induced Miller, Taylor, and Symington to abandon their invention and recur to their previous avocations.

In 1801 Lord Dundas employed Symington to construct a steamboat propelled by an engine on Watt's plan, "having one cylinder placed horizontally, and the piston, with a stroke of four feet in length, was jointed at the extremity, and attached to a connecting rod, with a crank at one end, turning a paddle-wheel, placed in a well-hole at the stern of the vessel, which has two rudders, one on each side of the cavity in which the paddle-wheel was placed." This vessel was named the *Charlotte Dundas*, and answered its purpose—that of towing vessels on the Forth and Clyde canal—completely, but, as usual, a storm of prejudice had to be encountered. The proprietors of the canal objected to the boat, alleging that the "wash" occasioned by the paddle-wheel would injure the banks of the canal. In the course of the next year the celebrated Fulton, who had been for some time in England, went to Scotland and visited Symington, who made several trips up and down the canal, and fully explained every part of the boat and apparatus to Fulton, who observed that the objection of injuring the banks of small rivers and canals, which might apply to England, would have no force in America, where things were on a larger scale. Having made notes of all particulars, Fulton went to France, built a steam-boat, tried it on the Seine in 1803, and soon after went to America. It is a curious fact in the history of inventions that both the First Consul of the French Republic and the English people, then well acquainted with the use of the steam-engine, should have allowed this important discovery to slip through their fingers. Fulton, however, had no doubt of the importance of the invention, and pursued it with a tenacity thoroughly American. In 1805 he applied to Messrs. Boulton and Watt to make a steam-engine, and applied it to a boat built in America. This was the *Clermont*—the wheels and machinery were on Symington's plan, propelled by Watt's engine. A speed of five miles an hour was attained; and from this time Fulton continued to construct larger boats, and applied to Boulton and Watt for more and more powerful engines.

These efforts in America excited much attention in this country. In 1812 Henry Bell, of Glasgow, started the *Comet* to ply for goods and passengers on the Clyde, between Glasgow and Helensburgh. This boat only attained the same speed as the American

Clermont—five miles an hour. From this date the improvement in the construction of steamboats and marine engines was comparatively rapid. The side-wheel system superseded the stern-wheel and in 1814 Boulton and Watt first applied two engines to a small boat on the Clyde. In 1819-20 four steamers were working between Dover and Calais; and by 1821 a line of steamboats was running between London and Leith. Meanwhile steam had been introduced into the Royal Navy, and Maudslay and Field had applied a valve for improving the expansive action of steam in the cylinder. In 1825 William Jolliffe, in conjunction with Bessell and Hall, established the General Steam Navigation Company, and built two vessels of between five and six hundred tons burthen. These vessels were intended to ply between London and Cadiz and London and St. Petersburg, but the company considered the project of Jolliffe as rash, and restricted their operations to the British Channel and the German Ocean.

In the memoir of the late Charles Wye Williams I find that about the year 1819 he—with the intention, originally, of assisting Mr. John Oldham, the engineer of the Bank of Ireland, and subsequently of the Bank of England—turned his attention to steam navigation, chiefly with the object of introducing Mr. Oldham's patent feathering paddles, which, after numerous modifications, became known as "Morgan's wheel." Mr. Williams consulted with the late Mr. A. Manby, of the Horseley Ironworks, and thence was produced a small steam-engine with two oscillating cylinders, the first of its kind and the precursor of all those which have since been so extensively used on rivers and at sea, by John Penn and other engineers. These engines, with a pair of Oldham's feathering paddles, were adapted to a whale-boat, at the Ring's End Foundry, Dublin, by Mr. Charles Manby (Hon. Sec. Inst. C.E.), and the success was so great as to lead to the formation of a steam company for the conveyance of passengers and goods between Liverpool and Dublin; and the company built, in 1823, the steamers *City of Dublin* and *Town of Liverpool*, each of 300 tons burthen. Mr. Williams was denounced as a bold and rash man to commence such a speculation with two ships. However, as it turned out, there was a call for more capital and ships, and four additional steamers were laid down, viz. the *Hibernia*, *Britannia*, *Manchester*, and *Leeds*. This growth of steam property caused the firm of Williams and Co. to merge into the firm of the "City of Dublin Steam Packet Company." At a later date Mr. Williams, in conjunction with Mr. Carleton, launched the famous Peninsular and Oriental Steam Navigation Company.

Rapid progress was now made in the construction

of marine engines. To obviate the inconvenience of the incrustation of boilers by the deposit of salt, Hall, of Dartford, introduced the system of surface condensation, while Maudslay and Field, in 1825, invented and patented their brine pumps, and Thomas Howard, of Rotherhithe, invented a refrigerator for pursuing the old system of condensation by jet. The next great event in the history of steam navigation was the crossing of the Atlantic by the *Great Western*, in 1838. This enterprise was due to the spirit of a Bristol company, with Brunel as their consulting engineer. Considerable difficulty was experienced in inducing engineers to attempt the construction of marine engines of sufficient power to drive a ship of 1240 tons burthen. Messrs. Maudslay and Field, however, undertook the work, and constructed a pair of engines on the side-lever principle, each of 210 horse-power, with cylinders 73 inches in diameter, and 7 feet stroke, making 15 strokes per minute. At her first trial on the Thames, the vessel went twelve miles per hour, and on the 8th April, 1838, started on her first voyage from Bristol, under the command of Captain Hosken, with seven passengers, 50 tons of goods, and 500 tons of coals, and reached New York on Monday, the 23rd April, thus accomplishing a distance of 3000 miles in thirteen days and ten hours. The success of this experiment, which surpassed the most sanguine expectations of its promoters, opened the eyes of the world to the possible extension of ocean steam navigation. The famous Cunard line from Liverpool to Boston was designed for carrying the mails, and started with four fast vessels of about 1000 tons and 450 horse-power each. This was followed by the Royal Mail Company, for carrying the mails between England and the West Indies, starting with twelve vessels of somewhat similar dimensions. The radical defect of these early steamships was the enormous weight of the engines, and the great space required by them, which rendered it difficult for them to carry any great amount of cargo beyond the passengers. This serious inconvenience led to the devotion of much ingenuity to the improvement of marine engines. Messrs. Seawards were the first to introduce engines wherein side levers were dispensed with, and the power applied directly from the piston to turn the paddle-wheel shaft. This system was modified by Miller, who was very successful in obtaining high rates of speed, and the long-standing objection of extra friction was got rid of by adopting the vibrating cylinders described in Trevithick and Vivian's patent in 1802, patented by Witty in 1813, and by Manby in 1821, by whom the first engines of this kind were constructed. Other improvements were adopted, and again improved upon by Maudslay and Field, Spiller,

Penn and Barnes, Miller, Seaward, Napier, Manby, Fairbairn, Hall, Rennie, and many other able men who turned their attention to the extension and improvement of steam navigation.

Just as the paddle-wheel was about to demonstrate its power to contend with the Atlantic waves, a rival propeller—destined ultimately to supersede it for ocean-going ships—sprang into existence. It was said by the late Sir John Rennie that "the first idea of stern-propelling was very probably suggested by the movement of fishes, whose chief propelling power exists in the tail, as also from the common and ancient practice of sculling a boat from the stern."

Be this as it may, rude notions of a screw propeller had long floated in ingenious minds. Shorter, Napier, Tredgold, and Brown tried and described the action of propellers of various shapes applied to different parts of a vessel. Cameron, Woodcroft, Lowe, Ericson, and others, patented screw-propellers; but nothing of positive value was effected until the year 1836, when the late Sir Francis Pettit Smith—since affectionately known as "Screw" Smith—obtained a patent for the application of a screw to propel vessels by placing it in that part of the stern of the vessel called the "dead wood." He accordingly built a small vessel thirty-four feet long, and made experiments with her on the Thames. With this little boat he achieved a speed of seven or eight miles an hour, and then tried her in a seaway. The Ship Propelling Company was now formed, and, under the direction of Smith, the *Archimedes* was designed by Pascoe, built at London by Whimshurst, and fitted with engines and machinery by Rennie. At first the propeller consisted of a single-threaded screw; but this not answering very well, another screw was soon adopted with two threads opposite to each other. The *Archimedes* was a success. She obtained a great velocity through the water, and proved herself an admirable sea-boat.

The success of the screw propeller was now demonstrated, and although vessels constructed on this system failed for awhile to accomplish the speed attained by those driven by the paddle-wheel, their superior power in a rough sea—since demonstrated beyond all possible question—induced the construction of the *Rattler*. Subsequently to this the *Fairy*, a Royal yacht, displayed the power of the screw in producing speed—this little boat of 260 tons burthen achieving 15¾ miles per hour through the water.

Coincident with these improvements in the machinery of navigation, a new material was introduced for the construction of vessels. Hitherto birch bark, bull-hide, and wood had been the chief materials employed in making ships, but in 1820-21 Aaron Manby constructed, at Horseley, near Birmingham, a wrought-iron boat of 120 feet length and 18 feet beam. This vessel, propelled by Oldham's feathering paddle-wheels, was built for the purpose of plying on the river Seine, and was navigated across the Channel by the late Sir Charles Napier. This boat continued to ply between Paris and Havre for many years, and although for a while superseded by other and more powerful boats, survived to wear out her engines, and, being fitted with new ones, held her own on the Seine for a long period. Notwithstanding the success of the *Aaron Manby*, the art of iron shipbuilding developed slowly, and it was not until the fifth decade of the present century that ironships came into general use, since when it has been decided to build steamships of no other material.

While these great demands were being made upon the iron industry of the country, an important modification was introduced into the method of smelting iron. The low furnaces of the Middle Ages had long since been superseded by the blast-furnace, and coke had supplemented charcoal in the important work of reducing iron ore. Powerful blowing engines had been used, but hitherto they had been employed simply in forcing through the tuyeres atmospheric air at its ordinary temperature. In the first volume of the "Transactions of the Institution of Civil Engineers" is a noteworthy paper communicated by

J. B. Neilson on the hot-air blast. In 1836 this gentleman writes to the president—"About seven years ago an ironworker, well known in this neighbourhood, asked me if I thought it possible to purify the air blown into blast-furnaces, in a manner similar to that in which carbureted hydrogen gas is purified; and from this gentleman's conversation I perceived that he imagined the presence of sulphur in the air to be the cause of blast-furnaces working irregularly, and making bad iron in the summer months. Subsequently to this conversation, which had in some measure directed my thoughts to the subject of blast-furnaces, I received information that one of the Muirkirk iron furnaces, situated at a considerable distance from the engine, did not work so well as the others; which led me to conjecture that the friction of the air, in passing along the pipe, prevented an equal volume of the air getting to the distant furnace as to the one which is situated close by the engine. I at once came to the conclusion that by heating the air at the distant furnace I should increase its volume in the ratio of the known law, that air and gases expand as 448 + temperature. In prosecuting the experiment which this idea suggested, circumstances, however, became apparent to me which induced the belief on my part that heating the air introduced for supporting combustion into air-furnaces materially increased its efficiency in this respect." The hot-blast came immediately into operation, and Mr. Neilson supplemented his paper by some remarks which now read curiously enough.

"Were the hot-blast generally adopted, the saving to the country in the article of coal would be immense. In Britain about 700,000 tons of iron are made annually, of which 50,000 tons only are produced in Scotland; on these 50,000 tons my invention would save in the process of manufacture 200,000 tons of coal annually. In England the saving would be in proportion to the strength and quality of the coal, and cannot be computed at less than 1,520,000 tons annually, and taking the price of coals at the low rate of *four shillings per ton* a yearly saving of £296,000 sterling would be effected."

It was indeed high time that a saving in the production of iron was effected, for a revolution was at hand, destined to transfer the carrying trade of the country from Brindley's canals and the magnificent highways designed by Telford to the iron roads now accepted as the ordinary means of transit.

The history of great discoveries reveals two salient peculiarities. First is the curious fact that at certain epochs the world becomes, as it were, ripe for the reception of great truths. From its four corners civilization addresses itself to the task of supplying the recently discovered want. Inventors of various nationalities advance by different roads and distinct means towards the great object in view. Investigators working in entire independence of each other arrive almost simultaneously at the same conclusion.

It would seem as if the human mind underwent periodical upheavings, and that outcrops of the same stratum of thought occurred in different localities. Instances without number may be cited—among others, those of Hooke and Newton, touching the law of the inverse square, of Watt, Cavendish, and Lavoisier, on the composition of air and water, and of Adams and Leverrier in the discovery of the planet Neptune. It is by no means clear who invented gunpowder, and the merit of first printing by movable types is hotly disputed. The history of chemistry abounds with illustrations of the law of simultaneous discovery. Without citing well-worn cases, I may quote a triple one. About twelve years ago the isomerism among the alcohols was simultaneously discovered in three separate countries by three independent sets of investigators in quest of entirely distinct objects: in Germany by Kolbe, in England by Wanklyn and Erlenmeyer, and in Paris by Wurtz and Friedel.

The second peculiarity is that no sooner is one class of mechanism brought to perfection than it is superseded by a fresh application of forces. Wind and water mills were no sooner perfected and fitted with the admirable mechanism invented by Smeaton, Arkwright, and Hargreaves, than Watt introduced steam as the great motive power. Archery had just attained its most perfect development when gunpowder was discovered. The arts of attack and defence of fortified places have seen many mutations. Fortresses hitherto deemed impregnable were reduced by line and rule on the method of trenches introduced by the Turks and improved by Vauban, and a siege was deemed a mere matter of time when the experience of Silistria, Kars, and Sevastopol proved that plain earthworks could hold their own when revetements of solid masonry must infallibly have given way. The art of building and manœuvring sailing ships had been reduced to a science, in the case of the famous yacht *America,* just as steam was superseding sailing ships altogether. Postal service had achieved perfection when the electric telegraph was invented, and roads and coaches had been brought to the highest pitch of efficiency at the very moment when railways were to revolutionize the face of the world. But however the merit of England in great inventions may be shared by other countries, this latter is unquestionably and indisputably her own.

About the commencement of the present century a

wild, eccentric man, named Trevithick—who had acquired some celebrity in the West of England as a mining engineer—succeeded in producing locomotive engines. In conjunction with Vivian and Blenkinsop he proposed ribbed wheels, with nails or bosses for the purpose of enabling the engine to ascend steep inclines. Previously to this date, rails or tramways had been made at various collieries throughout the kingdom, and flanges had come into almost common use. Dr. Robison, James Watt, his assistant Murdoch, and other inventors had calculated the possibilities of introducing locomotives on common roads, but the high-pressure engine was by the best authorities considered unsafe. Undeterred by these considerations, Trevithick and Vivian constructed a locomotive engine for the Merthyr Tydvil Railway. Working by adhesion alone, this engine, which "consisted of one high-pressure cylinder, with a fly-wheel and four bearing wheels—two of which were turned by the action of the piston—produced a velocity of five miles per hour dragging a load of fifteen tons." Unluckily for Trevithick, one of his engines exploded, and an accident which would have been deemed a mere trifle at the present day, and the costs whereof would have been calmly carried to the profit and loss account, sufficed—at the barbarous period referred to —to arrest the career of inventive genius for a time;

but in 1811 Blenkinsop took out a patent "for using rails having teeth like a rack in them, into which wheels having corresponding teeth were worked by the engine, thus securing the engine against slipping." This dèparture from the principle of adhesion was ignored by Blackett, who in 1813 resumed Trevithick's original plan, and "constructed an engine which worked by adhesion alone upon the rails at the Wylam Colliery at Newcastle." At this hour a man was prepared to crystallize by the power of his genins these crude efforts into a practical shape.

A keen, honest Northumbrian—the worthy father of a more worthy son—had advanced by this date to the position of engine-wright to Killingworth Colliery. Engaged during his leisure hours in superintending the education of his son, and in helping him to make a sun-dial by the aid of Ferguson's "Astronomy," George Stephenson bent his main energies towards the construction of a locomotive. This extraordinary man, who reached the age of eighteen without being able to read or write, had, in the following fourteen years, not only contrived to pull together a fair "scratch education," but had so greatly distinguished himself by his successful treatment of an obstinate Newcomen pumping-engine as to have acquired the *sobriquet* of the "engine doctor." Continually making improvements in locomotives, Stephenson took out patents, in conjunction with Dodd in 1815, and with Losh in 1816, and their productions were found equal, in 1820, to drawing coal trains at the rate of seven or eight miles per hour over the cast-iron edge rails recently introduced and patented by Birkenshaw.

The Hetton and the Stockton and Darlington Railways made by Stephenson were opened about 1825, and contained all the recent improvements in flanged wheels and wrought-iron rails. The first locomotive which ran on the Stockton and Darlington Railway is, I believe, still preserved as a valuable relic, and regarded with much veneration by the natives of Darlington. James had already foreseen the development of the locomotive, and in 1815 published a letter, proposing railways as a regular mode of communication; but it was not till the Liverpool and Manchester Railway Company obtained their first Act in 1826—leaving the tractive power to be employed an open question—that the locomotive excited general public attention. The company employed Messrs. Walker and Rastrick to report on the northern railways, and these gentlemen favoured the employment of stationary engines, while Stephenson and Rennie strongly advocated the introduction of the locomotive. Under these circumstances, the company offered a reward of five hundred guineas for the best locomotive engine. The result of the trial of the competing engines in 1829 electrified the world. The "Rocket," made by the Stephensons, attained the undreamt-of speed of twenty-five miles an hour, and decided the tractive question at once; and the Liverpool and Manchester was opened in 1830, Mr. Huskisson proving the first victim to the iron-horse. Interesting in itself, and deeply valuable for the lessons conveyed by it, is the record of the fanatical opposition brought to bear against the new system. That powerful and gloomy giant known as Vested Interest arose in his might, and contested the ground inch by inch. Landowners rose in arms against Stephenson and his works, and professional engineers denounced him as a quack, and his scheme as the most absurd "that ever entered into the head of man to conceive." Innumerable objections, practical and sentimental, were advanced. The railways would cut up the country, deform the face of Nature, burn up the crops, and throw entire districts out of cultivation. Cattle would be frightened to death, pheasants smoked out, the noble and important pursuit of fox-hunting interfered with, and the country generally would, to use the time-honoured sentence, "go to the devil." How far these profound vaticinations have been realized, the present state of England and English industry can testify.

Conscious of the disadvantage of a defective education, George Stephenson determined that his successor should suffer from no such drawback, and made the training of his son the object of his earnest solicitude. No narrative can be more touching than that of the studious evenings passed by father and son together after the labours of the day. A severe course of study prepared the young man to render his father most valuable assistance not only in the great railway controversy, but in the actual construction of the famous locomotive which established their reputation.

Taking with his father a prominent part in the construction of the English railway system, Robert Stephenson did not confine himself entirely to the ordinary work of a railway engineer. As a builder of stupendous bridges on a new and original plan, he acquired a high rank. The tubular bridge across the St. Lawrence at Montreal, and the Britannia Bridge, across the Menai Straits, remain as enduring monuments to his splendid genius. In 1855 he was elected president of the Institution of Civil Engineers, a post which he filled with such ability as to reflect honour both upon himself and the distinguished body over which he presided. A most endearing trait in his character was his loving admiration for his great parent. In the course of his presidential address he said: "It is my great pride to remember that whatever may have been done, and however extensive may have been my own connection with railway development, all I know, and all I have done, are primarily due to the parent whose memory I cherish and revere."

Another remarkable instance of the hereditary transmission of engineering genius occurred in the case of the Brunels. Sir Mark Isambard Brunel made his mark in several branches of engineering science, notably in the invention of the celebrated block machinery, and in the general introduction of bands of thin hoop-iron between courses of brickwork—an important improvement which has been extensively used ever since—but his name is more particularly identified with the Thames Tunnel—a stupendous work previously proposed and commenced by Trevithick, but subsequently abandoned. The difficulties encountered in the construction of this tunnel were of a nature to test to the utmost the perseverance and ingenuity of the constructor. By the invention of the famous shield, Brunel exhibited his fertility of resource, and by the completion of a work, then unique in its character, placed his name for ever on the roll of illustrious engineers.

During this great development of engineering genius the Institution of Civil Engineers had waxed mighty in the land. The institution was uniformly fortunate in the choice of its officials, but in the early days of its existence, under the presidency of Telford and the secretaryship of James Jones—to whom much of the credit of organizing the society is due—the finances failed to exhibit a prosperous aspect. The usual struggle for existence occurred. Many secretaries were appointed, among whom is found the name of Captain (afterwards Colonel) Stoddart—one of the Central Asian pioneers, who at Bokhara suffered the fate often imposed upon travellers by barbarous nations.

The name of Arthur Aikin—one of the founders of the Geological Society, the originator of the idea of the Zoological Gardens, the first president of the Chemical Society, and the famous secretary of the Society of Arts—also figures as honorary secretary to the Institution of Civil Engineers. After the death of Telford—who was interred in Westminster Abbey—James Walker was called to the presidential chair in 1835, and it was under the presidency of this celebrated engineer that the constitution of the society underwent a revolution, brought about mainly by the exertions of Mr. Charles (now Colonel) Manby. Mr. Thomas Webster (now Q.C.) held the appointment of secretary from 1836 to 1839, but on being nominated assistant to Judge Maule he asked his friend Mr. Manby to undertake his secretarial duties for a time. In 1839 Mr. Manby was appointed to the position, and at once put his shoulder to the wheel. In securing the services of this gentleman as secretary, the Institution was singularly fortunate, inasmuch as he not only possessed the true organizing faculty necessary to restore to the Institution its lost vitality, but was so happily situated as to be enabled to give a large portion of time to his labour of love. Under his care the society speedily gained strength, and has since asserted its existence with undiminished vigour. Fourteen years ago, Colonel Manby, whose exertions in the formation of an Engineer and Railway Volunteer Staff Corps have recently been gracefully acknowledged by the Indian Government, and whose works—many of which were undertaken in conjunction with the lamented John Robinson McClean—have met with ample recognition by foreign Governments, relinquished the post of acting secretary for the honorary dignity, since which date the duties of secretaryship have been admirably fulfilled by Mr. James Forrest, to whose courtesy I am indebted for much of the material of this sketch.

One of the principal changes brought about by Colonel Manby was the alteration of the term of presidentship. Feeling that the occupation of the chair for a long term of years by one individual, however distinguished, was prejudicial to the true interests of the society, he succeeded in inducing Mr. James Walker to resign the presidency in 1845, since which date the presidents have been elected annually, although it is a custom of the Institution to confer on its chief officer the honour of one re-election.

Since this important alteration in the constitution of the Society, only one president—Sir John Rennie—who sat from 1845 to 1848, has occupied the chair for more than two years.

Without any design to expand the present sketch beyond its proper limits, I find it difficult to pass over without special notice the names of the distinguished men who have filled the presidential chair of the Institution of Civil Engineers. In 1846 Sir John Rennie, on his elevation to the dignity of president, delivered that remarkable address to which I, in common with all subsequent writers on engineering, am largely indebted for many important and interesting particulars. In the course of this admirable specimen of comprehensive arrangement and lucid exposition, the president alluded to the railway work already done, and "the mania for new lines, which has exceeded all former precedent. 1901 miles have been already executed on the narrow gauge, 274 on the broad gauge; 614 miles are in progress of construction, and projects for 20,687 miles were actually introduced into Parliament last session, representing a capital of £350,000,000. Of these projects Acts of Parliament have been passed for 3573 miles, requiring a capital of £129,229,767." Only twenty-eight years have passed since these words were spoken, and the United Kingdom now boasts over 15,000 miles of railway, representing a capital of £600,000,000 sterling.

Sir John Rennie was succeeded by a man whose innate genius for mechanics had been developed by a course of severe training, and brought into prominence by a fortunate incident of which he took full advantage. After working under Sir Samuel Bentham at Portsmouth, young Joshua Field was brought up to the Admiralty at Whitehall to assist in the drawing department. At this period Mr. (afterwards Sir Isambard) Brunel was engaged on the famous block machinery then in process of construction by Maudslay. The latter gentleman requiring some assistance in drawing, applied to Sir Samuel Bentham to recommend him a competent draughtsman, when Sir Samuel and Mr. Goodrich strongly recommended young Field, who acquitted himself so well as to induce a permanent connection with Mr. Maudslay, whose partner he subsequently became. The famous house of Maudslay and Field has left its mark on the history of mechanical engineering. Besides occupying the first rank in the construction of marine engines, the house distinguished itself by its saw machinery, corn-mills, and mint machinery, and more especially by the construction of the first shield used in making the

Thames Tunnel. To Mr. Field, in conjunction with Mr. Henry Robinson Palmer, Mr. William Nicholson Maudslay, Mr. James Jones, Mr. Charles Collinge, and Mr. James Ashwell, belongs the honour of founding the Institution of Civil Engineers.

During the presidentships of Rennie and Field raged the "battle of the gauges." On either side of this great question were ranged the engineering giants of the day. The broad gauge—already adopted on the Great Western Railway—was warmly advocated by the younger Brunel, an engineer of brilliant and daring genius, who, albeit his conceptions rarely produced pecuniary success, yet acquired well-merited renown by the grandeur of his inspirations, and left behind him the reputation of one whose splendid failures were perhaps more instructive, and possibly more valuable, to mankind than the positive achievements of successful mediocrity. In the forefront of the opposing battalion stood the younger Stephenson, whose well-balanced intellect discerned at once the importance of carrying out great undertakings at a cost which should not entail ruin upon shareholders in order to enhance the reputation of the engineer. The result of this great conflict is now a matter of history, and the inclination now shown — wherever fresh ground is opened—to reduce the gauge to far narrower limits than 4 feet 8½ inches, demonstrates the solidity of judgment displayed by the great Northumbrian.

In 1850 Sir William Cubitt became president of the Institution. The career of this great engineer is one among many instances of gradual development. A miller's son with a taste for construction commenced by repairing the machinery of the mill, was subsequently apprenticed to a joiner, and tried to make a machine for splitting hides. This, although a failure, showed so much ingenuity, that the young man was taken into partnership by an agricultural machine maker. After inventing the self-regulating windmill sails, Cubitt commenced the construction of machines for draining marshes, and ultimately achieved extraordinary success in drainage works, canal making, and the construction of docks at Cardiff and Middlesborough. Turning his attention to railways, he—as engineer-in-chief — constructed the South-Eastern Railway, "where he adopted the bold scheme of employing a monster charge of 18,000 lb. of gunpowder for blowing down the face of the Round Down Cliff, between Folkestone and Dover, and then constructing the line of railway along the beach, with a tunnel beneath the Shakespeare Cliff." To the ear of the malefactor the name of Cubitt had an awful sound, as that of the inventor of the treadmill.

The chair was now successively filled by two

hydraulic engineers of the highest rank. James Meadows Rendel, after acquiring considerable reputation by his success in bridge building, devoted his attention more particularly to the construction of harbours and docks. Among his achievements may be enumerated the Birkenhead Docks, the new docks at Grimsby, and the Great Western Docks at Plymouth. Here he first introduced the method of construction since employed with so much success at the great harbours of Holyhead and Portland. In each of these great works many natural obstacles were overcome. At Grimsby the works were projected far out upon the mud-banks of the river Humber, entirely beyond low-water mark, and great difficulty was experienced in laying the foundations, owing to the treacherous nature of the substratum.

Born in the same year—1799—as Mr. Rendel, and succeeding him as president in 1854, James Simpson had previously turned his energies to the construction of waterworks, and designed and executed in 1828 at the Chelsea Waterworks his first filter bed, which had an area of about one acre, and proved so completely successful that no material alteration has been made in the system of filtration since that time. During the course of a long and prosperous career, Mr. Simpson constructed the works at Seething Wells and designed the extensive works for bringing to Bristol the springs and streams of the Mendip Hills. He also designed and executed the works for supplying Aberdeen with water taken from the river Dee, about twenty miles above the city, and, indeed, may be said to have made this department of engineering science peculiarly his own.

From 1856, when Robert Stephenson became president, down to the present day, the chair has been chiefly occupied by railway engineers. Stephenson was succeeded by Joseph Locke, who has been styled the third great leader of the engineering world, the two first places being conceded to Stephenson and Brunel. Singularly enough, these three great engineers were born within two years of each other, and within a similar space quitted the scene of their labours. One of the most salient characteristics of Mr. Locke was his keen appreciation of economy; he may indeed be said to have made his reputation by constructing the Warrington and Birmingham—then designated the Grand Junction Railway—within the estimate, at a cost of between £14,000 and £15,000 per mile. The commercial world was attracted by this valuable result, and Joseph Locke's reputation as an economical engineer assured him the direction of many great undertakings. He achieved much good work by discouraging the introduction of engines of various forms and by various makers on the same line, and by insisting on a system of uniformity in order to insure economy and promptitude in repairs. Mr. Locke left no monumental works behind him, but he has left a *monumentum ære perennius* in the hearts of grateful shareholders who have drawn dividends from his lines, while the ambitious labours of his rivals reduced them to the verge of impecuniosity.

Only last year the engineering world deplored the loss of John Robinson McClean, who became president in 1864. This gentleman, who was a son of the late Francis McClean, of Belfast, was born in that city in 1813, and was educated at the Royal Academical Institution. At the age of twenty-one he went to Glasgow, where his career was exceedingly brilliant. Studying for two sessions under Professors Thomson, Meikleham, and Sir W. Jackson Hooker, Mr. McClean obtained high honours in the classes of mathematics and natural philosophy, and at the same time pursued practical studies in mining engineering and surveying. On the completion of his university career, he entered the office of Messrs. Walker and Burges, civil engineers, 23, Great George Street, Westminster, and remained with them until 1844. During his stay with these gentlemen, Mr. McClean assisted in preparing the surveys and contract drawings of the improvements in Belfast Harbour, and other important public works undertaken by Mr. Walker; but in 1844 the rising young engineer determined to assume the independent exercise of the profession in which he afterwards took an active and distinguished part. In the very inception of his independent career he became the engineer-in-chief of the Furness Railways, and from that time forward was intimately associated with the great public works of that remarkable district, including the Barrow Harbour, Barrow Docks (which rival the famous docks at Birkenhead), graving-docks, railways, and other works. The modern history of Barrow-in-Furness is a record of rapid development unparalleled in the annals of industry. Hæmatite ore had long been known to exist in large quantities in this remote corner of Lancashire, but the development of the iron mines of Furness dates from the introduction of the railway system.

The growth of Mr. McClean's fortunes more than kept pace with the sudden extension of railways. Born at the very nick of time, he found himself in the possession of his full powers at the moment when the railway system—like a young giant—stretched forth its iron arms towards every point of the compass. Never was opportunity more readily seized. Pursuing his advantage with unfailing energy and untiring industry, Mr. McClean soon found himself in the foremost rank of his profession. He did not confine himself to the construction of railways, for when an agitation was commenced about the polluted state of the Thames, which, in 1849, was becoming full of sewage, and engineers were invited by the Metropolitan Commissioners of Sewers to send in plans for the drainage of London, the rising man failed not to contribute his scheme, and had the satisfaction of finding it most favourably viewed by the Commissioners, who considered it "the best conceived and most practicable scheme submitted to them." In 1849 Mr. McClean received into partnership Mr. F. C. Stillman, and the new firm at once engaged in the construction of the South Staffordshire Railway and branches, the Birmingham, Wolverhampton, and Dudley Railway, the Staffordshire and Worcestershire Canal Reservoirs, and the South Staffordshire Waterworks, supplying water to a population of nearly half a million.

In the year of the first Great International Exhibition, Mr. McClean carried out extensive works in Paris, and, on the death of Mr. Walker, was appointed Government engineer to the harbours of Dover, Alderney, and St. Catherine's, the Plymouth Breakwater, and the Shovel Rock Fort at Plymouth. During the next fifteen years the successful engineer enjoyed the full tide of popularity. He was at once consulting engineer to the Birmingham Canal Navigation and the Bute Docks at Cardiff, and engineer to the Surrey

Commercial Docks, the Tottenham and Hampstead Junction Railway, the Bristol and Portishead Pier and Railway, the Cannock Chase and Wolverhampton Railway, the Furness and Midland Railway, the Ryde Pier Company, and numerous other public works in Great Britain. He also held the post of consulting engineer to the Lemberg-Czernowitz Austrian Railway and the South-Eastern of Portugal Railway, and was, moreover, a fellow of several scientific societies.

Mr. McClean was preceded in the chair by Mr. George Parker Bidder—the bosom friend of Robert Stephenson—and by Sir John Hawkshaw. The career of George Bidder affords a peculiar instance of the triumph of method. The famous "calculating boy" has invariably disclaimed the possession of any extraordinary amount of memory, and has openly stated that a certain degree of proficiency in the art of mental calculation is within the reach of almost every one. In a remarkable paper on mental calculation, read by Mr. Bidder before the Institution of Civil Engineers in the year 1856, he explained with singular lucidity and happiness of illustration the operations performed by his mind while at work upon figures, and insisted very strongly on his favourite doctrine—that mental arithmetic can be taught like anything else.

The whole course of his argument is against the necessity for original genius, and in favour of the theory that the slow and gradual acquirement and the orderly arrangement of facts are the principal qualities demanded of the mental calculator.

He proceeds thus:—

"I do not, however, mean to say that it ought to be taught, or that it is desirable to attempt to teach it, to the extent to which I have been enabled to carry it. I have sacrificed years of labour, I have striven with much perseverance, to obtain and to retain a power or mastery over numbers which will probably, at all times, be as rare as is its utility in the ordinary affairs of life. Far be it from me, however, to say that it has been of little use to me. Undoubtedly the acquirement has attracted towards me a degree of notice, which has ended in raising me from the position of a common labourer, in which I was born, to that of being able to address you as one of the vice-presidents of this distinguished Society. But, as I have already said, I am not about to lay before you any abbreviated process of calculation; there are no "royal roads" to mental arithmetic. Whoever wishes to achieve proficiency in that, as in any other branch of science, will only succeed by years of labour and of patient application. In short, in the solution of any arithmetical question, however simple or complicated, every mental process must be analogous to that which is indicated in working out algebraical formulæ. No one step can be omitted; but all and every one must be taken up one after another, in such consecutive order, that if reduced to paper the process might appear prolix, complicated, and inexpeditious, although it is actually arranged with a view of affording relief to the memory. And here let me say, that the exercise of the memory is the only real strain on the mind, and which limits the extent to which mental calculation may be carried. It may be imagined that this is somewhat inconsistent with my previous observation that I possess no extraordinary power of memory. But it must be borne in mind that my memory is the limit by which my mental powers are restricted; and that the processes I pursue are all adopted, simply with a view of relieving the registering powers of the mind, *i.e.* the memory.

"I can perhaps convey to you no stronger view of this subject than by mentioning, that, were my powers of registration at all equal to the powers of reasoning or execution, I should have no difficulty, in an inconceivably short space of time, in composing a voluminous table of logarithms; but the power of registration limits the power of calculation, and, as I said before, it is only with great labour and stress of mind that mental calculation can be carried on beyond a certain extent. Now, for instance, suppose that I had to multiply 89 by 73, I should say instantly 6497;

if I read the figures written out before me I could not express a result more correctly, or more rapidly; this facility has, however, tended to deceive me, for I fancied that I possessed a multiplication table up to 100 times 100, and, when in full practice, even beyond that; but I was in error; the fact is that I go through the entire operation of the computation in that short interval of time which it takes me to announce the result to you. I multiply 80 by 70, 80 by 3; 9 by 70, and 9 by 3; which will be the whole of the process as expressed algebraically, and then I add them up in what appears to be merely an instant of time. This is done without labour to the mind; and I can do any quantity of the same sort of calculation without any labour, and can continue it for a long period; but when the number of figures increases, the strain on the mind is augmented in a very rapid ratio. As compared with the operation on paper in multiplying three figures by three figures, you have three lines of four figures each, or twelve figures in the process to be added up; in multiplying six figures into six figures you have six lines of seven figures, or forty-two figures to be added up. The time, therefore, in registration on paper will be as 12 to 42. But the process in the mind is different. Not only have I that additional number of facts to create, but they must be imprinted on the mind. The impressions to be made are more in number, they are also more varied, and the impression required is so much deeper, that instead of being like 3 or 4 to 1, it is something like 16 to 1. Instead of increasing by the square, I believe it increases by the fourth power. I do not pretend to say that it can be expressed mathematically, but the ratio increases so rapidly that it soon limits the useful effect of mental calculation. As a great effort, I have multiplied twelve places of figures by twelve places of figures; but that has required much time, and was a great strain upon the mind. Therefore, in stating my conviction that mental arithmetic could be taught, I would desire it to be understood, that the limits within which it may be usefully and properly applied should be restricted to multiplying three figures by three figures. Up to that extent, I believe it may be taught with considerable facility, and will be received by young minds, so disposed, quite as easily as the ordinary rules of arithmetic."

In 1862 Sir John Hawkshaw became president. During a highly successful career this gentleman has been engaged on many works of the first magnitude, among which may be cited the Lancashire and Yorkshire Railway, the Charing Cross Railway, and Londonderry Bridge. Sir John Hawkshaw also acquired great reputation by the resource displayed by him on the failure of the Middle Level sluice at St. Germans, near Lynn, where, instead of constructing a new sluice, he invented and erected syphons for the drainage of the district. Sir John Hawkshaw is an engineer of advanced ideas, and is a warm advocate of the Anglo-French tunnel under the Channel.

In 1866 Mr. McClean was succeeded by Mr. John Fowler, an engineer of the first rank, who has constructed lines in nearly every part of England, the Great Northern and Western systems in Ireland, the Metropolitan Railway, and numerous other railways in and around London.

Between 1868 and the date of writing, the chair has been occupied by four engineers of the highest distinction. Charles Hutton Gregory—a son of Dr. Gregory, the distinguished Professor of Mathematics at the Royal Academy, Woolwich—was brought up in the works of Messrs. Bramah and Co., and was early in life appointed the resident engineer of the Croydon Railway. He subsequently became connected with the Bristol and Exeter, and all the lines of railway within that district, and has latterly been generally consulted by the Crown Agents for the Colonies.

Mr. Charles Blacker Vignoles holds one of the oldest commissions now extant in the British army. He was on active service in Spain, and distinguished himself in a "forlorn hope," whence he was lucky enough to escape with a whole skin. On the advent of "piping times of peace," he turned his mathematical knowledge to good account, and, as became the grandson of old Dr. Hutton, he embraced the career of a civil engineer. Mr. Vignoles constructed many notable works in England, and also took his share in the parliamentary fights of the last generation. He then turned his attention to Russia, where he made several lines of railway, and the famous Kieff suspension bridge. Mr. Vignoles has also had a large share in constructing the railway system of South America. Mr. Thomas Hawksley—who succeeded Mr. Vignoles as President of the Institution of Civil Engineers—commenced life as a surveyor, but speedily attained celebrity as a surveyor for water and gas, and has designed and constructed many important works at Nottingham, Liverpool, and other places. In the present year Mr. Hawksley gave place to Mr. Thomas Elliot Harrison. This gentleman was brought up in the office of Robert Stephenson, in whose estimation he stood very high on account of his clearness of judgment and fertility of resource. Mr. Harrison has acquired deserved celebrity by the construction of the High-Level bridge at Newcastle, and of the docks and other great works connected with the North-Eastern Railway.

The illustrious roll of presidents, and the record of their achievements, form after all but a small part of the history of the Institution of Civil Engineers. Among the members are Sir William Armstrong, who achieved celebrity by the invention of the hydraulic crane and the gun which is called after him; his great rival in the manufacture of ordnance, Sir Joseph Whitworth, the founder of the famous Whitworth scholarships; Dr. C. W. Siemens, whose researches in metallurgy have acquired for him a world-wide reputation; James Abernethy, James Brunlees, J. F. Bateman, Joseph Bazalgette, Sir William Fairbairn, Isaac Lowthian Bell, Sir George Elliot, William Menelaus, and many more able engineers and inventors, to mention all of whom would be a lengthy task.

Suffice it to say that during the last half-century the genius of English engineers has displayed its power in every region of either hemisphere. While the vast peninsula of Hindostan was being knit together by iron bonds, an enterprising band of English engineers laid the foundation of the railway system of South America. The success of the Mauá Railway—designed and constructed by Edward Brainerd Webb—opened the eyes of the Brazilians to the value of railway communication in a country of such "magnificent distances" that railroads are the only possible roads. From Brazil the desire for railways spread to the River Plate, where many important railways have been made, and others are still in course of construction by Mr. Webb and other eminent engineers. On the transandine side of the continent much has also been done in facilitating means of communication and opening up to commerce the immense resources of South America. The Peruvian Government is constructing, under the advice of Mr. Edward Woods, about 500 miles of railway, and the Chilian Government about 300 miles. Railways have also been introduced into Japan; but the offer of a railway to the Emperor of China has not yet met with a cordial acceptance. Nearer home many great works have been undertaken, among which may be cited the Amsterdam Ship Canal—now being executed under the direction of Sir John Hawkshaw and Mr. Dirks—and large additions to the dock accommodations of Liverpool. To these last it was originally proposed to add several of Mr. Edwin Clark's hydraulic docks; but the invention of the pneumatic floating dock by Messrs. Latimer Clark and Standsfield has led to the adoption of the newer and far more economical substitute.

It is gratifying to find that, in the great race of life, English engineers still hold their own, but it is also worthy of remark that the professors of an important and exclusively modern department of engineering have not hitherto been deemed worthy of the highest honours conferred by the Institution of Civil Engineers. Perhaps the existence of a "Society of Telegraphic Engineers" explains the seeming oversight; for, although no member of the army of electricians has yet occupied the post of President of the Institution of Civil Engineers, the society in Great George Street has shown no reluctance in taking to her bosom these professors of a new science. In fact the Institution is sufficiently catholic in its views, and opens its doors to no less than four classes of persons. Honorary members are "distinguished persons" not engaged in the practice of the profession. Among the fifteen honorary members are the Emperor of Brazil, the Prince of Wales, the Duke of Connaught, and General Todleben. The members number 793, and have already been—so far as space will permit—individually referred to. In addition to the actual members, 1295 associates are enrolled. These gentlemen are not necessarily civil engineers by profession, but must be qualified to concur with civil engineers in the advancement of professional knowledge, and moreover must, like the actual members, have attained the age of twenty-five years—a highly salutary regulation. Express provision is made for the admission of students, who must be between eighteen and twenty-six years of age, and must be or have been pupils of members or Associates of the Institution. At the present moment

289 Students are admitted to many of the most important privileges of membership on paying a subscription of £2 2*s*. per annum.

A few years since the Council of the Institution made an inquiry into the present system of educating engineers both at home and abroad, and elicited much valuable information ; but in consequence of a feeling among the members that it was better to let things alone, nothing was done. Experts on the Continent, as well as in England, expressed grave doubts concerning the advantage of a severe training in the sciences bearing upon the profession before engaging in its actual practice. In true English style, the systems adopted in France and Germany were decried as producing a race of great schoolboys, who knew nothing "practical," were childishly ignorant of mechanical engineering, and displayed at critical moments an utter absence of that fertility of resource which is one of the characteristics of the English engineer. This is all excellently well, but at the same time those Englishmen who have been contaminated by foreign influences may be excused if they decline to consider theoretical knowledge a positive drawback in the engineering or any other profession. Continued insistence on the virtues of the "practical man" is apt to render one weary of that overpraised individual. It is easy to admire his pluck, his resource, his handiness in overcoming difficulties, but it is now and then impossible to resist the conclusion that, if the practical man had possessed a little more scientific knowledge, he would have found fewer difficulties to overcome. The whole question appears to be mainly one of time. At first sight, it is of course dreadful to think of arriving at manhood without having acquired anything but theory; but, on the other hand, it is questionable whether the time invested in scientific study is not rapidly recouped when the young theorist is set to practical work. On the one hand is the fault into which the universities of Oxford and Cambridge have fallen, viz. that of keeping men at school till they are twenty-three years old, an age at which a man ought not only to have left school, but have acquired at least the power of doing work in some walk of life; while on the other is the obvious disadvantage of bringing up a race of half-educated youths, whose only chance of getting on in life is to blunder on from failure to failure, until success is achieved more by force of character than by constructive skill. Possibly the true technical education—like many other things—has yet to be discovered.

Members, associates, and students of the Institution are alike stimulated to exertion by many premiums and medals, for which ample funds have been provided by the Telford, Miller, and Howard bequests, and the Manby donation. Interesting proceedings take place at the ordinary meetings of the Society, which are often protracted over several sittings. The papers read are considered the property of the Institution, and for this or some other inexplicable reason, the press are severely enjoined not to publish any record of the proceedings beyond the official *précis* of the original paper presented to them by the Society. In many cases of great public interest this policy of restriction is severely felt. The grievance is not so much that only a *précis* of the original paper may be reported, but that the discussion is entirely reserved for the Transactions of the Society. A notable instance of the inconvenience occasioned by this rule occurred last year. A great debate was expected on a subject of the highest importance—no less than the break of gauge in India. I found the great room of the Institution crowded with eager debaters and anxious listeners. Mr. Thornton's able paper provoked a discussion which will long remain in my memory as one of the most remarkable for interest and vivacity that I have been privileged to witness. For months the public remained in a benighted state on the Indian railway question, simply because the publication of the discussion on the most interesting question before the engineering world was impossible, except through the ordinary official medium.

As for myself, I enjoyed the proceedings immensely, simply because I was not allowed to write about them, and my appreciation of the argumentative power and the opposite theories of the great engineers who entered the arena was not dimmed by the knowledge that work was then and there by me to be performed; but on leaving Great George Street, after each brilliant meeting, I could not help regretting that before the record of the discussions could reach the public eye the heat of battle would have passed away, and the Indian railway question—undergoing the fate of other questions—have crystallized into a lifeless thing of the past.

V.

THE CHEMICAL SOCIETY.

One of the first to recognize the truth that science has in modern times acquired a range not to be comprised by any one institution, the Society of Arts has ever been ready to assist the formation of any association having a special object, and has recently established special sections of its own, such as the Indian and the Chemical Section. Specialty is, indeed, one of the salient features of the nineteenth century. Special knowledge and special power are everywhere in demand. In law, in the arts, and more especially in science, the specialist is looked upon with a peculiarly favourable eye. Mankind gratefully acknowledges its obligations to the man who devotes his life to the attainment of perfect knowledge within a certain narrow sphere. Never was the "Jack of all trades and master of none" doctrine more implicitly received than at the present moment; and never was the "life-view" (as he calls it) of my friend Professor Engeström so generally accepted. The professor—who is constantly insisting that the aim and object of life cannot be too early decided upon and too rigorously adhered to—is fond of citing the instance of the famous grammarian who devoted his life to the dative case. Doubtless this scheme of life, leaving the world's work to be done by infinite division of labour, does not meet with much sympathy from old-fashioned people, who incline to the idea that more perfect manhood is achieved by a general student than by a narrow specialist. These well-meaning people urge that in olden times men were more many-sided than they now are, and that one individual might be a good soldier, sailor, lawyer, and politician, and therefore enjoy a fuller life than his descendant of to-day; but it behoves us to recollect that it was not difficult to know all that was to be learned four hundred years ago. The recorded wisdom of the western world might have easily been contained in a hundred tomes, and, with the exception of mathematics, science in its exact sense was unknown. Astronomy, struggling in the trammels of traditional cosmogonies, was largely mingled with astrology. Botany was confined to the enumeration of the properties of simples plucked under certain lunar influences. Chemistry was in the alchemical stage, busying itself with the elixir vitæ; and the metallurgy of the period consisted of researches into the imaginary transmutation of metals and the vain pursuit of the philosopher's stone.

During the last two centuries more advance in scientific knowledge has been made than during all the thousands of previous years, but it is during the present age that facilities of communicating thought and its results have led to the splitting up of the sciences into minute divisions and subdivisions. As lawyers have divided law until the pursuit of each narrow branch has become a distinct profession; as doctors have dissected the human body and divided it among them, one taking the eye, and another the ear, the brain, the heart, the lungs, the throat, or the stomach as his peculiar domain of research; so has the mantle of Friar Bacon or of Schwartz—fit representatives of the ancient alchemist or astrologer—been cut up into many fragments, and distributed among astronomers, naturalists, physiologists, botanists, geologists, physicists, metallurgists, palæontologists, and chemists.

The immense development of chemical research in this country by Davy, Dalton, and their contemporaries very naturally suggested the formation of a society having for its object the advancement of chemical science. It is true that the Royal Society was always ready to welcome the accomplished chemist, and it would argue slight knowledge of the history of chemistry to overlook the brilliant discoveries made in the laboratory of the Royal Institution, but it was, nevertheless, felt that a special society was needed for the encouragement of chemistry as distinguished from physics and other cognate sciences. It was thought that chemistry had at length grown big enough to have—like the ancestral O'Donoghue—a "boat of its own," and the important bearing of the newly-developed science upon the industry of the country was urged as a powerful and tempting argument in favour of stimulating chemical investigation. The honour of the initiative is due to Mr. Robert Warington, who convened a meeting for the purpose of taking into consideration the formation of a Chemical Society. The meeting was held in the well-known rooms of the Society of Arts on February 23rd, 1841. Among those present were the excellent and ubiquitous Mr. Arthur Aikin, W. R. Grove, Lyon Playfair, and Professor Graham, who occupied the chair. The formation of a Chemical Society having been resolved, the objects of the Society were declared to be the promotion of chemistry, and of those branches of science immediately connected with it, by the reading, discussion, and subsequent publication of original communications, and the formation of a chemical library and museum. The annual subscription of members resident within twenty miles of London was fixed at two pounds, and of those residing beyond that distance at one pound. Thomas Graham was elected the first president; J. T. Cooper, W. T. Brande, J. F. Daniell, and R. Phillips, vice-presidents. Arthur Aikin—still full of energy—was appointed treasurer; and Robert Warington and E. F. Teschemacher, secretaries.

A council was appointed, the names of seventy-seven gentlemen who had become members were then read, and the Society adjourned until Tuesday, the 13th April. The Society now continued to meet regularly from time to time, and between 1841 and 1847 published three volumes of Memoirs and Reports of Proceedings. At the latter date the members numbered between two and three hundred, and it was therefore considered desirable that steps should be taken for obtaining a Royal Charter of Incorporation, which was granted in the following year. In accordance with this document, the Chemical Society consists of Fellows, honorary and foreign Members, and Associates. The Fellows elect out of their own body a governing council consisting of a president, four or more vice-presidents, a treasurer, two secretaries, a foreign secretary, and twelve other Fellows. At the present moment the presidential chair is filled by Dr.

Odling, and among the vice-presidents who have filled the office of president are found the familiar names of Brodie, Frankland, Hofmann, Lyon Playfair, and Williamson. Mr. W. H. Perkin and Dr. Russell are the efficient secretaries; Dr. Hugo Miller fills the post of foreign secretary, and Mr. Abel acts as treasurer. Other magnates of the chemical world figure in the list of the council, notably Drs. Roscoe, Maxwell Simpson, Stenhouse, and Armstrong. The post of librarian and editor of the Society's journal—a duty much increased of late by the incorporation of translations of foreign papers—is ably filled by Mr. Henry Watts, whose tremendous "Dictionary" is a lasting witness to the way in which he performs his valuable work. Candidates for admission to the Society are proposed on a form of recommendation subscribed by five Fellows of the Society at least, three of whom recommend the neophyte from "personal knowledge," while the remaining two may recommend from "general knowledge"—whatever that precise form of knowledge may be worth. After being balloted for and duly elected by three-fourths of the voters, the new Fellow pays an admission fee of two pounds and his first year's subscription or life-composition, and is then received into the bosom of the association by the president, who, taking him by the hand, says, "Mr. ——, I do, by the authority and in the name of the Chemical Society, admit you a Fellow thereof." At the present moment the Fellows number about eight hundred. Of the Associate—a species of "free-list subscriber"—only one instance exists. The number of foreign Members is limited to forty, but on this list are found many of the most illustrious names in the history of chemistry. First on the roll stands Balard, the discoverer of bromine; and next to him Berthelot, who contributed to chemical science the Syntheses of Formiates, of Alcohol, and of Acetylene. Boussingault, famous by his researches into the Chemistry of Vegetation, follows next, and precedes the illustrious Bunsen, whose name is rendered dear to the scientific world by the invention of the Bunsen burner, by the perfection of gas analysis, and by the discovery of cæsium, and rubidium, and the spectrum analysis. Next follows Cahours, whose researches in potato spirit, and determination—in conjunction with Hofmann—of the phosphorus bases, are fresh in the memory; Canizzaro, made famous by the Synthesis of Aromatic Alcohols, and his considerations on Atomic Weights from Specific Heat; and Chevreul, identified with the Chemistry of Fats and the Theory of Colours. The name of Deville recalls aluminium; and that of Dumas the Theory of Types and Organic Analysis. Many other famous chemists are on this remarkable list — notably

Wöhler, of Göttingen, who, so long ago as 1828, established the Synthesis of Urea, and Wurtz, the discoverer of Glycol and Ethylamine; Stas, well known by his researches on Atomic Weights; and Kekulé, of Bonn, identified with Atomicity and Thiacetic Acid. Two great names now challenge attention. Kolbe, of Leipzig, celebrated by the Electrolysis of Fatty Acids—by the Synthesis of Formic Acid from nascent Hydrogen and Carbonic Acid—by the Synthesis of Oxalate of Sodium from Carbonic Acid and Sodium, and by the Theory of Isomeric Alcohols. Pasteur has not only written his name in the history of chemistry by his discovery of optical differences in Amylic Alcohol and in Tartaric Acid, but has become famous in physiological controversy by his experiments in biogenesis. Conducted in a truly philosophical spirit, these famous experiments form an epoch in the long contest between the advocates and opponents of the theory of spontaneous generation.

From its foundation to the present day, the Chemical Society has done much good solid work. Recorded among its proceedings are many papers which have left their mark on the history of chemistry. From its earliest days the Society has shown a keen appreciation of Teutonic research, and has devoted much time and pains to the translation of papers by eminent German chemists. In 1841 translations were read of the papers on "Cacodyl Compounds," contributed by Professor Bunsen, then of Marburg. During the next two years Dr. Stenhouse read many papers before the Chemical Society. Aniline now attracted the attention of Muspratt and Hofmann—in whose laboratory Perkin was destined to discover the commercial value of mauve. Hofmann himself communicated papers on the Metamorphoses of Indigo, and on Styrole.

In 1845 Hofmann pursued his researches on aniline, and in 1848, while professor at the Royal College of Chemistry, contributed to the Society his researches on the Volatile Bases, including the papers on the "Action of Cyanogen on Aniline, Toluidine, and Cumidine," on the "Action of Iodine on Aniline," and on the "Action of Chloride, Bromide, and Iodide of Cyanogen on Aniline." While Hofmann was pursuing this line of investigation, Kolbe and Frankland were making researches into the nature of the Organic Radicals, and Liebig contributed papers from time to time. In 1857 Church and Perkin communicated the results of their study of "some new colouring matters, Derivatives of Dinitrobenzole, etc.," and Mr. Perkin followed this by a paper on the "Action of Cyanogen on Naphthalamine." At this period Dr. Lyon Playfair also sent in papers on the "Nitro-Prussides," and other subjects.

In 1858 Wanklyn communicated a paper on the Synthesis of Propionic Acid, followed at a later date by the Synthesis of Propione, and in 1863, then working in conjunction with Erlenmeyer, produced Hexylic Compounds from Mannite.

In the pages of the *Journal of the Chemical Society*, Kopp has recorded his investigations into the Specific Heat of Solid Bodies, and Kolbe his Synthesis of Oxalic Acids and his Prognosis of New Alcohols and Aldehydes.

The late Ernest Chapman read papers on many subjects—in particular on Limited Oxidation. In 1867 a paper describing the Ammonia Process of Water Analysis was communicated by Wanklyn, Chapman, and Smith; and was followed in the next year by the rival system of Frankland and Armstrong, which brought about a vigorous controversy. Dr. Frankland, working in conjunction with the late Mr. Duppa, also produced some excellent papers on Ethide of Boron and on the Reduction of Oxalic Ether to Leucic Ether by the action of Zinc-Ethyl. The year 1868 was marked by Dr. Siemens' paper on the Regenerative Gas Furnace as applied to the manufacture of cast steel; and more recently Isaac Lowthian Bell contributed a valuable paper on the Chemistry of the Blast-furnace.

The Chemical Society is one of those highly favoured

bodies which, like the Royal Society and the Geological Society, are permitted to occupy a portion of Burlington House. A magnificent suite of rooms is allotted to it. There is a handsome library, admirably appointed, and enriched by a fine collection of chemical works, and regular files of English and foreign scientific periodicals. Adjoining the library is the inevitable tea-room, without which the domain of no scientific society is complete. Beneath these apartments is the great room of the society, fitted up with benches in ascending order, like those of an ordinary lecture-room. Behind a long table, more or less encumbered with chemical specimens and apparatus, sit the president and the two secretaries—the two latter gentlemen being charged with the onerous duty of reading papers in the absence of their authors. The presence of a number of ballot-boxes reveals the fact that several gentlemen recommended on the basis of "personal" or "general" knowledge are up for election; and the reception of many recently-elected Fellows, according to the form prescribed, indicates that the Chemical Society is adding largely to its list of members. This is a cheering sign, but my spirits are slightly dashed when I observe the extreme youth of many among the audience. As the names of the visitors—of whom each Fellow may introduce two—are read aloud, I find that their number does not account for the remarkable preponderance of young gentlemen. On inquiry I find that these must, therefore, be actual Fellows. I naturally experience some little surprise at this discovery, as I was once inclined—in the innocence of my heart—to attribute a certain distinction to the mystic letters F.C.S. Now, no human being is more inclined to encourage youth, and more disposed to regret its loss, than myself. It has long been an article of my creed that when a man is able to do good work, he is old enough to be entrusted with it, and I never lose an opportunity of insisting that in life the "time" is not, as musicians say, "taken quickly enough," but I find it difficult to resist the conviction that many of the juvenile Fellows of the Chemical Society cannot possibly have attained any higher rank than that of students or of assistants to lecturers. I may be mistaken. The young gentlemen referred to may have attained eminence in the chemical world, or the letters F.C.S. may not be intended to convey any grave significance, but I confess that I am puzzled.

Elections over, the reading of papers is proceeded with. Many of these are important, and a particularly interesting account of researches in Phenol is read by Dr. Armstrong, the chemical professor of the London Institution. Time passes quickly, and the attention given to the business of the evening is perfectly warranted by its engrossing character. Much revolving these things, I at length emerge into Piccadilly admiring the youth of the Fellows of the Chemical Society, and wondering why a powerful body like this, possessing a fine library, has yet no museum of its own.

VI.

THE DEPARTMENT OF SCIENCE AND ART.

It would be difficult to find a more curious and instructive illustration of the growth of English institutions than the Science and Art Department of the Committee of Council on Education. In other ignorant countries—such as France, for instance—there is always a Minister of Public Instruction, a sort of chief schoolmaster, who is supposed to look after the education of the million; but in this country it was long deemed unnecessary to create a minister without any perceptible functions. Five-and-twenty years ago there was little talk about education, and, so far as the many were concerned, there was none. The reports of Government inspectors have clearly demonstrated that the so-called teaching of the National Schools practically amounted to nothing, and could hardly be designated education without provoking a laugh. Since then much has been done in the way of educating the people, and the Lord President of the Council has been called upon to fulfil in England the duties assigned abroad to the Minister of Public Instruction. This procedure is intensely English. A brand new office, created to supply a fresh and growing want, would hardly have suited the insular genius. We had a Lord President of the Council whose duty apparently was to perform presidential instead of, as was said of the archdeacon, "archidiaconal" functions. He was paid a good round salary, and should be made to work for it. Hence education is represented in the Upper House by the Lord President, and in the Commons by the Vice-President of the Council, to the great delight of Englishmen, who love to explain to the "intelligent foreigner" that, although they have no special Minister of Instruction, they yet have the thing under another name.

The Department of Science and Art was formed out of three more or less elementary bodies—the Department of Practical Art, the Royal College of Chemistry, and the Royal School of Mines, whereof the second has been long since absorbed by the third, which, although now included under the General Department, enjoys a distinct existence, a separate constitution, and a clearly defined income of its own. I would fain have discoursed in separate essays on the rise, progress, and ultimate destiny of these several institutions, but this Gordian knot is all too toughly interlaced to yield to my blunted penknife. So far as my limited powers go I will endeavour to set forth the peculiar functions of each body, but dissever them I neither must nor may. All are now linked together under the broad title of the Department of Science and Art. The Department was regularly constituted in 1853 by a Minute of the Treasury, in consequence of the representations of the Board of Trade (under whose jurisdiction the Department of Practical Art, above alluded to, was at that time included), was placed under the Committee of Council on Education, and during the first six years of its existence was mainly employed in reorganizing the system of Art Instruction.

Without going into the particulars of the purchase of the Gore House Estate—bought partly with the surplus funds left in the hands of the Royal Commissioners for the Exhibition of 1851—it may be sufficient to state that the late Prince Consort induced the Government of Lord Palmerston to build the well-known "Brompton Boilers," at a cost of £15,000, the Commissioners giving the land, for the purpose—in the first place—of exhibiting the collection of pictures presented to the country by Mr. Sheepshanks on the express condition that the donor should see a building erected to receive his gift. Subsequent additions to the "Boilers" afforded room for the pictures till then exhibited in Marlborough House, to which the old Schools of Design held at Somerset House and elsewhere were transferred for a while—ultimately to find their home in South Kensington. A Parliamentary grant of £10,000 was devoted to this latter purpose, and South Kensington became the fulcrum of the Art teaching of the country. Unwilling that the metropolis should absorb all the advantages of artistic instruction, Mr. Henry Cole, the Secretary of the Department, undertook the onerous task of extending these benefits to the entire country through the instrumentality of parish and other local schools. The old Schools of Design had been encouraged after a peculiar fashion. Grants of money were made to certain towns on the condition that they should themselves furnish an equal sum to that contributed by the State; for instance, Manchester received £600 on condition that that city should add an equal sum. This system was exposed to many disadvantages. In the first place, the Government grants were difficult to get. Kidderminster strove in vain for a grant on the ground that the manufacture of carpets required a School of Design, and Stourbridge pleaded her glass manufactures without success, while in those cities where schools actually existed the Government almost invariably got the worst of the bargain. Local contributions came in slowly. In many cases it was found impossible to keep faith with the Government, and the results were lamentably incommensurate with the outlay of public money. It was at once seen that until a properly organized staff of teachers was formed nothing valid could be done, and energetic measures were taken to supply this need. A body of properly certificated teachers was formed. These instructors received at first a certain salary, coupled with an additional remuneration, according to the results of their teaching, shown by their pupils under examination. Ultimately this plan—which was not without merit of its own—was superseded by the system of "payment for results."

For the first six years of its existence, from 1853 to 1859, the Department found Art easier to manage than Science, and experienced very great difficulty in organizing the scientific branch. Until the year 1859, elementary instruction in science was hardly attainable by the artisan. It is true that some of the principal mechanics' institutions scattered over the great towns had from time to time "popular" lectures on scientific subjects, illustrated frequently by experiments, diagrams, or specimens, but these lectures rarely extended to systematic courses. In very few institutions were any classes for collective instruction, scarcely any had laboratories, and whatever collections of natural objects existed were almost always ill-arranged and incomplete, even for the purposes of very limited instruction. A few exceptions to this description existed in Glasgow, Edinburgh, Manchester, Liverpool, and London, but in the smaller towns, and in manufacturing and rural districts, no instruction was to be acquired. Various attempts had been made to remedy this state of things. The creation of a Central Science School in the metropolis was strongly recommended, but has not been carried out to this day. Meanwhile attempts were made to kindle into life what were called Trade Schools.

These proved such a conspicuous failure, that when the late Lord Salisbury became Lord President of the Council, he resolved that he would either abolish the word Science out of the title of the department, or he would cause some science to be given to the country. Accordingly, about the year 1859, certain principles were laid down which enabled the Department to encourage the teaching of certain sciences bearing upon industry. These principles have since been carried much further. Stated briefly and broadly, the system now at work is, that any locality that pleases may establish a Science School or class. It may be held—in the words of Mr. Cole—in a garret, or may be held in a cellar, without concerning the Department in any way, unless a grant in aid of building be asked for—when certain conditions are insisted on. The teachers are appointed by the local committees, and must have proved their competency by examination. The local committee simply notifies the Department that it has constituted itself, and may then proceed to teach any one or all of the twenty-three sciences enumerated in the Science Directory, and may request that at a certain period of the year the students be examined.

The examination is conducted by papers sent down from the office in London, and on the results the teachers get payments, and the students prizes. Payments are made on behalf of those who are interpreted to belong to the artisan class—clearly defined in the Science Directory—but the prizes are open to all. The theory is that the artisan class pay moderate fees, and the middle classes larger fees. Gratuitous instruction is now abolished, the payment of fees being insisted upon as a qualification for undergoing examination. Teachers are paid by results, that is, so much per student of the artisan class that passes examination successfully. The payments are in the following proportions:—£1 for every second class, in either the elementary or the advanced stage; £2 for a first class in either of these stages, or for a second class in honours, and £4 for a first class in honours. The object of this system of remuneration is to directly encourage the formation of a class of teachers of elementary science, and to stimulate them to activity by granting payment for "results" alone. The success of this plan has been rapid. In 1860, 500 persons were under instruction in nine schools; in 1867, 10,230 persons were under instruction in 212 schools; while in 1870, 34,283 persons were taught in 799 schools. From 1870 to 1872 the rate of increase slackened, as no more than 36,783 persons are reported as having been instructed during the latter year. Fourteen of these obtained gold, twenty silver, and thirty-three bronze medals, while 5931 received prizes. Between 1872 and 1873 a tremendous leap was made, the number reported under instruction in May, 1873, being 48,546, to whom sixteen gold, eighteen silver, and thirty-four bronze medals, and 7215 prizes were given.

The expenditure of the Science and Art Department during the financial year 1872-73, exclusive of the vote for the Geological Survey, amounted to £209,117 2*s*. 2*d*., and with the addition of £21,385 1*s*. granted for that important object, reached the grand total of £230,502 3*s*. 2*d*. In the succeeding financial year 1873-74, the total expenditure reached £262,503, showing an increase of £32,000 16*s*. 10*d*., and in the current year, dating from the 1st April, 1874, to the 31st March, 1875, it is proposed to devote an increase of £15,667 to the Department of Science and Art bringing up the estimates to £278,170. This sum, £278,170, is distributed as follows:—

Administration of Science and Art Department	£5,422
Schools of Science and Art	120,110
Purchases and Circulation	23,682
South Kensington Museum	38,024
Services common to the several divisions ...	28,177
Branch Museum, Bethnal Green	5,810
School of Mines and Geological Museum ...	8,998
Edinburgh Museum	9,824
Royal Dublin Society	1,823
Botanic Gardens (Dublin)	2,148
Leinster Lawn (Dublin)	200
Museum of Natural History	1,672
Library (Dublin)	1,677
Royal College of Science (Dublin)	6,883
Royal Hibernian Academy	300
Royal Zoological Society of Ireland	500
Geological Survey of United Kingdom ...	22,920

Without going into minute details of increase and decrease, it may be said briefly that £168 is saved on the item Administration, £605 on Purchases and Circulation, £372 on the South Kensington Museum, and £445 on the Royal Dublin Society. An increase of £877 is devoted to Services Common to both Departments, £240 to Bethnal Green, £592 to the

Edinburgh Museum, and £253 to the Geological Survey. It is, however, gratifying to record that £15,550, or nearly the entire net increase, is devoted to the Schools of Science and Art, raising this item from £104,560 in 1873-74 to £120,110 in 1874-75. The total increase under this head is put down at £15,550, but a saving on the School of Naval Architecture (now removed to Greenwich) of £310, and a deduction of £50 from scholarships, bring the net amount disposable for other branches up to £15,910, distributed thus:—

SCHOOLS OF SCIENCE AND ART.

Grants in Aid to Schools of Science and Art.	Increase.		Total.
Science	£7,500	...	£40,500
Salaries of National Art Training Schools	300	...	2,100
Maintenance of Students	—	...	2,800
Public Elementary Schools	4,000	...	15,500
Artisans attending Night Classes ...	900	...	17,500
National Scholarships, etc.	100	...	1,600
Local Secretaries	300	...	1,300
Preparation for Papers, etc., for Examinations	1,150	...	6,750
Inspection and Examination	960	...	12,310
Local Committees	500	...	3,800
Prizes	800	...	7,800
Scholarships	—	...	750
Grants for Examples	400	...	5,400
Building Grants...	—	...	2,000
	£15,910		£120,110

Some of these items may speak for themselves, but others will need some slight explanation. The sum of £6,750 charged under the head of Preparation of Papers, etc., for Examination is distributed among the following gentlemen, of whom the Examiners in Art are Sir F. Grant, R.A., Sir M. Digby Wyatt, C. W. Cope, R.A., R. Redgrave, R.A., F. R. Pickersgill, R.A., H. Weekes, R.A., J. C. Horsley, R.A., F. Leighton, R.A., and J. Marshall, F.R.S., with assistants. In Science, the examination papers are prepared by Professors Tyndall, Frankland, Huxley, and Percy, with their able staff of assistants.

The papers prepared by these high authorities are sent down into the country, and the pupils are examined them in presence of the committee, the teacher being rigorously excluded from the building, and by the result of these papers the pass degrees or honours, gold, silver, and bronze medals and other prizes, are awarded to the pupils, and the capitation fees assigned to the teachers. The sum which has been increased to £40,500 in the present estimates, and is put down as "Science," is entirely devoted to the payment of science teachers "by results."

Few will cavil at the gross amount distributed among the science teachers of the country, especially when regard is had to the immense amount of work done for it. Capitation fees for successful pupils in the proportion of one, two, and four pounds per head, according to the degrees of efficiency exhibited under examination, may be satisfactory enough as "encouragement" to the teachers, but barely answer to the demand for sufficient remuneration for work done. As a stimulant to exertion the premium on results is well enough without doubt, but it holds out a prize not always to the swift, nor even to the strong, but often to the lucky. In writing on scientific subjects it is always well to eliminate the element of chance, if possible; but in the case of popular education it is not always possible to achieve this feat. Into scientific teaching chance enters largely. To begin with, the teacher may have dreary up-hill work. The district wherein he is called upon to lecture may be swayed by adverse influences. Noble pursuits, such as dog-fighting and nurr-and-spell, may hold out superior attractions to some, while cricket and skittles may deflect other pupils from the science class. Admitting that the absorbing influence of these truly British pastimes may be overcome, and a fair class attendance secured, the teacher still has to contend with numerous disadvantages. His pupils may be below even the average level of stupidity. He may talk and he may experiment, but if the material of his class be thoroughly dense his labours may prove vain. Another difficulty arises from those indolent or half-hearted students who, imagining that they have acquired the smattering they deem necessary, shirk the examination, the results of which alone entitle their pastor and master to remuneration.

Laziness and a childish fear of breaking down also help to deprive the master of his fair exhibit. Worse than all of these is a selfish indifferentism, which induces pupils to disregard the master's interests altogether so long as their own turn is served. Against all these adverse influences the Science teacher has to contend, and it therefore hardly seems fair to deny him all remuneration except by "results." As a proof of the injustice that frequently occurs, I may cite the case of a Science teacher who took high honours, and who yet by the "result" system only received £7 for a course of sixty experimental lectures in his first year of teaching, since when—during the last four or five years—he has delivered ninety lectures per annum, and has earned from £12 to £26 by each course. As this is by no means an isolated case, it would appear that the hard and fast line of payment "by results alone" may be advantageously departed from by granting teachers a small salary—say of £10 or £12 per annum—as a species of guarantee against actual dead loss of time. The large range of subjects included in the advanced stage of chemistry is also pointed out by the teachers as a special source of hardship. They declare that students are unable, within a reasonable time, to master the numerous obligatory subjects sufficiently well to face the examiner, and that therefore a vast amount of care and painstaking on the part of the master never has a chance of being recompensed either by pence or praise.

In order to set forth clearly what is at first sight not very distinct, I may say at once that the items previously enumerated include all that is done for Science by the Department as such, save and except the courses of instruction given for the express benefit of Science teachers. Art is taught directly to pupils at South Kensington, but Science is not—by the Department. There are laboratories at South Kensington where pupils and "Science Teachers in Training" receive instruction, but these are more particularly devoted to the School of Mines. No Science, then, is directly taught by the Department (which only encourages others to teach), except to the teachers themselves. Lectures are given in summer by the professors of chemistry, physics, and other branches, with the express object of enabling country teachers to obtain a knowledge of the latest discoveries and newest experiments. These lectures were commenced in 1869, were attended with great success, and have since become a regular part of the summer programme of the Department. It has been customary to afford such country teachers as have taught two years consecutively, and passed not less than thirty students each year, second-class railway fare to London, and £3 towards their expenses of living while there. For the future this arrangement will probably be modified in order to enable a certain number of teachers to stay long enough in London to undergo a course of instruction in teaching certain special subjects. Should this scheme be carried out, such teachers will receive 30*s*. per week instead of one payment of £3.

Science teachers, then, enjoy the privilege of attending these lectures on condition that they do their work thoroughly. They are required to make notes, to afterwards write out a complete report of each lecture, and also to take part in practical work. The reports are examined by the professors, and marks are awarded in accordance with the merit displayed. No less important is the practical teaching given in the laboratories, especially when it is recollected that the object of these courses is to enable teachers to give practical instruction in the several sciences. This plan has called into existence a system of tuition in practical science which has already borne good fruit. Students, instead of being confined to mere listening to lectures, are now taught to perform, and to assist in performing, experiments with their own hands. This system has produced a promising crop of students, of whom about forty-five are at present prosecuting their more advanced studies in the laboratories of the Royal School of Mines under the title of Science Teachers in Training. Time and space permit—for the present—the extension of this latter advantage to a limited number only, but it has been suggested that a most desirable improvement would be made by permitting such promising pupils as are in the habit of assisting their teachers in experiments to listen to the lectures at South Kensington.

While at work in their own classes the teachers are subject to visits from the Government inspectors, selected for the most part from the officers of the Royal Engineers. There can be no doubt as to the conscientiousness with which these gentleman discharge their duties, but it is possible that the number of inspectors is not sufficiently large, inasmuch as I am imformed that certain classes—not of the most obscure order—escape inspection for years together. A Science teacher of some experience tells me that for five years he was never once honoured with a visit of inspection, although his class is held at a well-known spot in the heart of London. Complaints of this kind indicate distinctly enough that the rank and file of

Science teachers do not feel very well satisfied at being placed under the inspection of a body of gentlemen who, although possessed of high scientific attainments, have had comparatively slight experience of actual teaching. Perhaps the teachers think that their future inspectors ought to be drawn from their own body—but this by the way.

Pupils are encouraged by the offer of a large number of Exhibitions, Scholarships, Medals, and Prizes. Among these the Royal Exhibitions to the School of Mines, the Whitworth Scholarships, the Royal Exhibitions to the Royal College, Dublin, and the privileges conferred on the gainer of a gold medal at the May Examination are the most important, but these are supplemented by many local and conditional prizes and exhibitions, grants for laboratories, etc. The whole system is now in fair working order, and during the last fifteen years has produced results as important as they were unexpected.

Having now sketched slightly the past and present of the famous Department of Science and Art, taken in its entirety, I may proceed to advert to those scientific institutions which combined with the Department of Practical Art to produce the vast network of Art and Science schools with which the country is rapidly becoming covered. It is true that the Royal College of Chemistry exists no longer as an actual corporation, but an account of scientific culture in England would, nevertheless, be incomplete without some notice of that institution.

Travellers down Oxford Street will observe a building now converted into a general Medical Council House, looking grimly enough at its neighbour, the Royal Orthopædic Hospital. This establishment—albeit financially a failure—has left no slight mark on the history of science. It was once called the Royal College of Chemistry, and during its short span of existence saw much notable work performed within its walls. The college was first established by a public meeting held in St. Martin's Place, on the 29th July, 1845. Form was given to the new institution by the election of a council and the appointment of certain executive officers. Rooms were next hired in George Street, Hanover Square, as laboratories, but it was soon found necessary to secure a more convenient and permanent habitation. Ultimately premises in Hanover Square, with a frontage to Oxford Street, were secured, and the most eminent architects and chemists were consulted as to the formation of an economical and convenient edifice, with the most efficient arrangements for the operations of the laboratory. On the 16th of June, 1846, the first stone of the building was laid by the late Prince Consort, the President of the college, who had already conferred immense benefit upon the college by persuading Dr. August Wilhelm Hofmann to preside over it. This celebrated chemist had commenced a brilliant career as assistant in the chemical laboratory of the University of Giessen. He subsequently held the appointment of Professor Extraordinary at the University of Bonn, but in 1845 forsook the banks of the Rhine for those of the Thames, and became Professor of the Royal College of Chemistry in London.

After filling this chair for several years, Dr. Hofmann—pending whose possible return Dr. Frankland accepted the post of provisional professor—was summoned to Germany to preside over the erection of new laboratories at Bonn and at Berlin, and was prevailed upon to remain in the Prussian capital—a resolution which it is dimly rumoured he has since had cause to regret. During his residence in London, Dr. Hofmann added greatly to his scientific reputation by carrying out his classical researches on ammonia—showing the successive replacement of hydrogen by various organic radicals—in the laboratory of the Royal College of Chemistry. He also, in conjunction with the eminent French chemist M. Cahours, discovered a remarkable series of phosphorus representatives of the compound ammonias. Meanwhile, a discovery of the utmost industrial importance was made in his laboratory. Perkin, in the course of some preliminary investigations into the possibility of producing artificial quinine, discovered the famous Perkin's mauve while oxidizing aniline with chromate of potash. This discovery brought its author into well-merited fame—albeit it was well known at the time—when mauve, if not discovered for the first time as a colour, was at least for the first time made commercially valuable—that the technical knowledge and enterprise of a dyer at the East end of London, who ably seconded the exertions of the chemist, contributed largely to the industrial value of these investigations.

Fortunately, or unfortunately, it was discovered, or thought, that successful philosophical investigation barely compensated for financial failure, and the Royal School of Chemistry became a doomed institution; not destined, however, to absolute extinction, but rather to absorption, as tottering principalities are sucked into the vortex of neighbouring empires. Pure science was in this case destined to cede the place to technical education. Again, under the auspices of the late Prince Consort a new and vigorous organization had sprung into active life, and becoming in its vigorous growth too large for its own habitation, acquired that of the dwindling College of Chemistry as a sort of scientific chapel of ease. The council of the college, despairing of success, handed over the building, valued at £3000, to the Government, on condition of a claim of some £500 being settled; and thus in 1853 the College of Chemistry became the laboratory of the Royal School of Mines, under the condition that it should retain its original designation.

The origin of the School of Mines lies deep down in the primary strata of technical education, and was due, in the first place, to the enterprise of the late Sir Henry de la Beche, in undertaking single-handed the Geological Survey of the United Kingdom; and, in the second, to the English habit of adapting existing institutions to immediate wants. As is well known, the survey undertaken at first by Sir Henry de la Beche, at his own cost, underwent a gradual expansion, and, as the value of the work became apparent, received more and more support from the State. In 1837 Lord Duncannon, Chief Commissioner of Woods and Forests, allotted apartments in Craig's Court to receive the collection which has since developed into the Museum of Practical Geology in Jermyn Street. In 1851, when the latter building was opened, the survey had assumed imposing proportions. Its working staff contained not only practical geologists and field-surveyors, but a naturalist, a mining surveyor, a mineralogist, a metallurgist, and a chemist.

In the same year numerous memorials, praying for

the establishment of a mining school, were addressed to the Government. It was urged that—though the value of the annual mineral produce of this country amounted to £28,000,000, equalling four-ninths of the total amount produced by the whole of Europe, and far exceeding that yielded by any other State—"the miners and metallurgists of the United Kingdom were unable to obtain that instruction in the theory and the practice of their calling, which had long been carefully provided for their foreign competitors in the mining colleges of France, Belgium, Prussia, Saxony, Austria, Spain, and Sweden, and the effect of which in all cases had been a marked increase in the economy, efficiency, and safety of mining operations."

The voice of the representatives of the mining interest was raised at the right moment. Finding ripe and ready to hand the complete nucleus of a mining school in the officers, laboratories, and collections of the Geological Survey, the Government lent a willing ear to the request of the memorialists. In 1851 the School of Mines was instituted, all its professors being, with one exception, officers of the Survey and Museum. The existing establishment was further utilized. Students were taught in the theatres and laboratories appertaining to the Museum; where, surrounded by specimens and models, they possessed every opportunity of profiting by the prescribed course of instruction. As has already been stated, the laboratories soon outgrew the resources of Jermyn Street and were transferred, firstly, to the Royal College of Chemistry, and, lastly, in 1872, to South Kensington. Certain parts of the work, however, are still done in Jermyn Street. Thus, while Messrs. Frankland, Huxley, Guthrie, and Goodeve — the lecturers on Chemistry, General Natural History, Physics, and Applied Mechanics—have transferred their habitat to South Kensington, Messrs. Warington Smyth, Percy, and Ramsay—the lecturers on Mining and Mineralogy, Metallurgy, and Geology—still pursue their labours amid the illustrative specimens with which the Museum of Practical Geology abounds. The School of Mines is governed by a Council of Professors, whose resolutions are carried into effect by the Registrar, Mr. Trenham Reeks. To the lectures given by this institution the public are admitted on payment of three or four pounds, according to the length of the course, and are granted certificates of attendance, but students wishing for certificates of proficiency are compelled to pass the examinations. Those, however, who desire an official certificate constituting them Associates of the Royal School of Mines are required to follow a course of study extending over three years, and to pay a sum of thirty pounds on entrance, or to make two annual payments of twenty pounds each, exclusive of laboratory fees. This plan of instruction, combining systematic courses of lectures, written and oral examinations, practical teaching in the laboratories and drawing office, and also—under certain conditions—field excursions, is of a thoroughly scientific and, withal, technical character, and is, perhaps, the best extant English representative of the admirable system of technical education in force in Germany, Switzerland, and France. For the first two years a general training is insisted upon, but after the second year pupils may attach themselves to any one of the three divisions prescribed, and may take a first-class in only one of these divisions if preferred. This very sound and practical plan of study commences in the first year with inorganic chemistry, with practice in the laboratory, and mechanical drawing. In the second year pupils are taught physics, with practice in the laboratory, applied mechanics with demonstrations, mechanical drawing and mineralogy.

Having completed these courses, pupils may in the third year "go out" in either of the three following divisions:—The Mining Division, comprising mining, assaying, and geology; the Metallurgical Division, trained to metallurgy in the laboratory; or the Geological Division, including natural history, with practice in the laboratory, geology, and palæontological demonstration. Although the course of instruction is spread over three years, persons may, if possessed of sufficient knowledge or industry, save time by getting through the whole and their examination in a couple of years, while those who have already mastered the subjects set down for the first two years may proceed to the courses of the third year by passing the final class examinations in those subjects.

It is hardly necessary to say that those persons who desire the title of Associate are the peculiar pride and care of the Royal School of Mines. Among these are the Royal Exhibitioners. There are nine Royal Exhibitions to the School of Mines, of the value of £50 each per annum. The holders are entitled to "free admission to all the lectures and the chemical and metallurgical laboratories" for three years, on condition of compliance with the rules, regular attendance, and the passing of the examinations required for the associateship. As a rule, three of these exhibitions become vacant every year, and are open for competition at the May examinations of the Science and Art Department, independently of the other prizes offered by that department. All persons over twenty-one years of age—excepting artisans and such persons as are paid upon under the "Science Directory," that is to say, broadly, persons whose income is under £200 per annum—are excluded from competing for the Royal Exhibitions. It is pleasing to record that these exhibitions have produced really good fruit. Many young men sprung from the true artisan class have won them well, and worn honourably the subsequently acquired title of Associate.

Apart from the Royal Exhibitioners and persons desiring associateship, many others are offered strong inducements to pursue the course of study prescribed by the institution. Those who have taken either a first or second-class certificate in "the advanced stage in any subject in Science at the exhibition held by the Science and Art Department, and who show that they are *bonâ fide* Science teachers, may attend the day lectures gratuitously, provided that they be examined in at least one subject, paying a fee for each examination of one pound per course." Officers of the Army and Navy, Her Majesty's consular and diplomatic officers, officers of the Crown at home on furlough, and acting mine agents and managers of mines are admitted to the lectures at half-price. Moreover, those who obtain a Queen's Gold Medal at the annual May examination of the Science and Art Department receive the privilege of attending all lectures and examinations free. Students of the Royal Schools of Mines compete for two scholarships of thirty pounds each, granted by H.R.H. the Prince of Wales as Duke of Cornwall, and thence called the

Cornwall Scholarships. Three Royal Scholarships, one of twenty-five pounds, and two of fifteen pounds each, are granted to students who stand highest on the list for first and second years of study. In addition to these prizes are the Edward Forbes, the De la Beche, and the Murchison medals and prizes.

In a thoroughly broad and catholic spirit the lectures—instead of being confined to high-class students—are thrown open to the public on payment of the sums previously mentioned, and the chemical and metallurgical laboratories are open to any person, whether attending the lectures or not, on payment of the following fees :—In the chemical laboratory twelve pounds for three months, nine for two months, and five for one month; and in the metallurgical laboratory fifteen pounds for three months, twelve pounds for two months, and seven pounds for one month.

Although the institution of a School of Mines was loudly enough called for nearly a quarter of a century ago, and since that date the inadequate supply of technical education in this country has been a favourite theme with educational reformers, the advantage of undergoing a special course of training with a view to acquiring the associateship of the Royal School of Mines—a distinction to which due regard is paid in allotting Government appointments—did not seem for nearly twenty years to attract the attention that it merited; but during the last four years a notable increase has taken place in this as in other classes of students. Thus, in the session 1870-71 the number of "Royal Exhibitioners and Students entering for one, two, or three years, with a view to become Associates," was only 15. In 1873-74 a great advance was made; 44 postulants for the degree of Associate having presented themselves. During the four years indicated a corresponding increase has taken place in the number of "students entering for special courses." In chemistry the number has arisen from 24 to 48, in physics from 15 to 40, in metallurgy from 4 to 14, and in applied mechanics from 5 to 14, and the fees paid by students rose from £720 5*s.* in 1870-71 to £1,554 16*s.* in 1873-74. These fees are for the most part distributed among the professors. The account for the past year has not been published, but I find that in 1872-73 the fees amounted to £1137 3*s.* 4*d.*, of which the professors received £995 0*s.* 1*d.*, the balance of £142 3*s.* 3*d.* being paid into the Exchequer. It will at once be recognized that the additional income arising from fees is necessary to afford anything like adequate remuneration to the able professors engaged, whose fixed salary as "lecturers" is only £200 per annum, except in the cases of the chemist and the metallurgist, who receive £300 each, and in that of Professor Ramsay, who, in addition to the appointment of geological lecturer, holds the directorship of the Geological Survey of the United Kingdom, worth £800 more.

Those who wander down Exhibition Road become aware of a handsome red-brick building, and—on the principle of taking things upon trust—believe it to be the South Kensington Museum. No belief can be more unfounded, as this structure really contains the lecture-rooms and laboratories of four of the departments of the School of Mines—chemistry, physiology, physics, and applied mechanics. On the several floors reign Professors Frankland, Huxley, Guthrie, and Goodeve. In a spacious theatre, admirably constructed, lighted, and moreover shielded from the light by a skilful arrangement of blinds, and fitted with well-constructed desks, Professor Frankland delivers his lectures on chemistry. Ascending a few flights of stairs, I discover the large resources at the command of the chemical section. Here are laboratories indeed. Rooms—many of them as yet far from sufficiently furnished—are set apart for the various departments of the chemical curriculum. Conspicuous among these are the "balance-rooms," for elementary and advanced students, rooms specially fitted for gas and water analyses, for combustions, and other processes in advanced chemistry. Strolling through these apartments, under the care of that earnest professor, Mr. Valentin, who gives practical instruction in chemistry, I find in every room evidences of sustained industry. Students of gas analysis are busily engaged in marking off metrical tubes, while others more advanced are engaged in the finer niceties of the analysis itself. Nothing is more agreeable to the truly scientific mind than this insistence on actual work. A chemist, or for that matter a physicist—to be worth his salt—must be able to construct his own apparatus. In the active exercise of his profession he will often be compelled to make—out of simple glass tubing—an apparatus for grand combustions, including the famous five-bulb invention of Baron Liebig. In London he can buy these things, or—at a certain sacrifice of time—have them made; but the genuine worker will save much time by making his apparatus himself, and besides this advantage will always get exactly what he wants. Passing next into a room devoted to distillation, I find myself in the midst of a busy scene. The professor pauses for a moment to observe that an indiarubber tube is not a proper part of an apparatus for distilling alcohol, and to recommend a glass tube deftly bent into the required curve, when we proceed into the laboratory for advanced students. This room is well fitted with quiet, silent workers, each at his table busily engaged in working out the higher problems of chemistry. One young gentleman is evolving chlorine in a fashion easily distinguishable by the nostrils, and comes in for a few remarks from his pastor and master, who devotes a few minutes to the removal of a cloud from the mind of that painstaking but unlucky student. From the advanced school I pass into the laboratory for young scholars, and am not a little surprised at the extreme youth of many of the occupants. Every place is occupied, and every youth, and a few no longer youths, are busily engaged. Clearly, good honest work is being done here, and on a system, the invention of which is, I believe, due to Mr. Valentin himself. The students are armed with his excellent books, and are working patiently through them. Not only is their work carefully checked by the professor and his two assistants, but the scholars are literally brought to book by an admirably arranged series of questions at the end of each chapter. This precaution is highly necessary, inasmuch as a scholar may blunder—by good luck and deft manipulation—through an experiment without thoroughly understanding and grasping its *rationale*. The plan of cross-questioning effectually disposes of this difficulty. No youth can possibly perform an experiment and stand the subsequent cross-examination unless he thoroughly comprehends what has been done. The students are working well.

Those who have not enjoyed the advantage of a previous course of lectures are put through a proper course of elementary experiments, and as soon as they have exhibited tolerable proficiency in "qualitative," are at once indulged in the more attractive "quantitative" analysis. Professor Valentin is not dissatisfied with his disciples, and is not inclined to include want of earnestness and energy among the defects of Young England. Germans are perhaps more anxious and imaginative by fits and starts, but English youth make up for the want of those qualities by their faculty of sustained exertion.

In the physical school Professor Guthrie is delivering a lecture on Electricity to a large class of students. This peculiar section is supplied with a perfect arsenal of appliances for performing experiments, many of them of the most costly kind. In this respect Professor Guthrie has enjoyed a certain advantage in being enabled to remove the splendid apparatus, accumulated during a series of years at the School of Mines, to South Kensington. Professor Goodeve's department (applied mechanics) is hardly so well off. The lecture-room is yet in the crude condition which, in the case of the chemical laboratories, called forth some time since a strong remonstrance from Dr. Frankland. To my great sorrow I find that the physiological course of Professor Huxley is over for this season; but although the students have sought other, if not fresher, woods and pastures new, the professor himself is discovered hard at work on some anatomical drawings. He is busy, but not too busy to deliver for the express benefit of Major Donnelly—the Government Inspector of the Science Department—and the writer, his views on "thorough" scientific teaching. Professor Huxley loves to make his students begin at the beginning. A thorough believer in human ignorance and stupidity, he takes utter and complete ignorance for granted.

Nothing can possibly be more agreeable for the student, who is not asked to know anything, but is simply required to pay attention to what is set before him. The system of teaching initiated by Professor Huxley is purely and simply after the manner of Euclid. No attempt is made to build an airy and showy superstructure upon a rickety and insecure foundation. Bit by bit, brick by brick, the edifice of physiological knowledge must be reared; and the student is not exhorted but compelled to lay each successive row of bricks for himself. "My system," saith the professor, "is very much that of Mr. Whackford Squeers—w-i-n-d-e-r—winder—go and clean it." Students are lectured and told about a thing, and then are at once set to dissect and prepare the specimen for themselves. Even then they prefer a formula, or a drawing to copy from, if they can find it in their memory; but Professor Huxley will have none of this. What he demands, and insists upon, is that they shall acquire a clear and distinct idea of "things," not a confused jumble of "hard words." The application of this positive mode of teaching—long since practised in chemistry—is in physiology due to Professor Huxley. Mere listening to lectures and taking of notes will never produce any true scientific knowledge. Students must learn to make the experiment. Carefully and painstakingly they—after the master has shown them the book—must turn over the leaves, and reveal, to their own vast improvement, the secrets of nature.

Professor Huxley's views on the admission of female students to the physiological course are sufficiently catholic. The example of Miss McConnish, who has become an accomplished demonstratrix in physiology, inspires the professor with a certain faith in the clearness and positivity of the female intellect. The great drawback to the instruction of ladies in the more recondite mysteries of physiology is found in the difficulty of lecturing to a mixed class of young persons of both sexes. It is no more difficult to lecture to a female than to a male class, but the objections to a mixed auditory will suggest themselves to all persons of ordinary refinement.

The physiological department is enriched by many beautiful specimens, and illustrated by a series of fossils culled from the immense repository at the Geological Museum in Jermyn Street, and moreover possesses the advantage of affording a view over the domain of South Kensington. The new Museum of Natural History is rising above its foundations, and from its ground plan appears likely to afford ample room for the specimens now crowded together in the British Museum. This latter institution must, as it appears, undergo a gradual process of disintegration. At the present moment it is a vast *omnium gatherum* of incongruous atoms. A collection commenced, probably enough, with an Indian god and a stuffed crocodile, has developed into a vast heterogeneous museum. Books and stuffed giraffes, elephants and rhinoceroses, Assyrian bricks, the Elgin marbles, Egyptian papyri, and a mineralogical collection, hardly "hang together," and it is comforting to find that at least one section will find its way to South Kensington.

One of the most interesting features of the School of Mines is found in the Lectures to Working Men. The institution of these lectures is due to the enlightened foresight of the Minister under whose instructions the school was founded, and who stipulated expressly that the professors should deliver annually, at a nominal admission fee, a course of lectures to working men. It was considered—and very properly considered—that an institution subsidized by the nation for the express object of affording a certain class of technical education, should contribute to a certain extent towards the great "national object of educating those who are prevented by circumstances from educating themselves." These lectures were commenced in 1851, and immediately attracted so large an attendance, and excited so much interest among the class for whose benefit they were instituted, that in the following year the officers of the School determined to increase their labours in this direction. The arrangement then made has continued in force ever since. Each professor gives a course of six lectures in alternate years, thus providing working men with an average of twenty-four instead of six lectures in each year.

The fee paid by the artisan is truly nominal. It is simply a registration fee of sixpence for each course of six lectures, giving the working man an opportunity of hearing science of the highest and most recent order discoursed upon in the very plainest English that the subject will admit of, by professors of the first rank, at the rate of one penny per lecture. A certain evening is announced for the distribution of tickets between the hours of seven and ten p.m.

Each applicant is required to bring his name, address, and occupation, written on a piece of paper, in return for which, and the sum of sixpence of the lawful money of the realm, he receives his ticket of admission to the particular course given. If any proof were needed of the avidity with which scientific information is coveted by the artisan, the rush for tickets on one of those evenings would amply supply it. Only six hundred tickets are or can be issued, the lecture theatre not affording accommodation for a greater number. The whole of these, and many more, are applied for on the evening prescribed; no chance exists of getting a ticket after that date, on which many a time and oft large numbers of applicants are sent empty away.

During the late session three courses of these lectures have been delivered. The first on Heat, by Professor Guthrie; the second on Metals, by Dr. Percy; and the third on Natural History, or rather "On the Phenomena of Life as Motion and Consciousness," by Professor Huxley. Feeling anxious to hear how Dr. Huxley will make the complex phenomena of nerve action clear to his auditors, I wend my way to Jermyn Street on one of those charming spring evenings, when a pleasant admixture of rain and hail makes existence delicious, and compels the traveller to warm himself with the reflection that, albeit he is wet and cold, he yet is an Englishman; that he loves the "Wild North-Easter," as Mr. Kingsley has instructed him to do; and that in the pursuit of Science he can afford to disregard climatic asperities, which matter little except to inferior beings. It wants twenty minutes to the appointed hour, and the happy possessors of tickets are arriving in great strength. The theatre is already nearly full, but the benches appear to possess a certain elastic property, and every corner is occupied. Having, probably, more to do than the fashionables at the Royal Institution, the working men do not arrive an entire hour before the time in order to secure the best seats, but the theatre is completely filled long before the clock strikes. I look around me at the audience, and I am content. He is here, this working man, whom I have so often sought and found not. His place is not usurped by smug clerks or dandy shopmen. In all his various forms and ages, from the keen-eyed apprentice to the experienced artisan, he is here—in force—this handicraftsman—this maker of things.

It is a silent audience. These men are evidently fresh from the workshop, striving to overcome the obliterating influences of a week of humdrum everyday occupation, and are burnishing up their memories touching the last lecture—not a few aiding these organs by note books. There is no well-bred hightoned chatter going on. Perhaps the silence is due to the absence of *Angot* caps and red opera cloaks and perhaps to the earnestness of the audience. Be this as it may—as the hands of the clock turn towards eight there is no perceptible rustling, hushing, and settling down. The silence simply becomes, if possible, a degree more profound than before. A burst of applause welcomes the professor, who has undertaken to explain, on this particular evening, "The Co-ordination of the Modes of Motion of Living Bodies with those of the Surrounding World." This title has, in truth, a tough look, but when manipulated by Professor Huxley proves eminently digestible. With admirable lucidity, and with an utter absence of "hard words," the lecturer proceeds to discourse upon the action of the nerve forces—as a distinct phenomenon from sensation or consciousness. Confining his remarks mainly to involuntary or—according to the more explicit terminology of Professor Huxley—reflex action, the lecturer dilates upon those mechanical movements of the body—such as sudden contraction—which are produced at once by the contact of external objects without any exercise of volition on the part of the patient. Clear, precise, and distinct in his description of nerve mechanics, the professor reserves a rare sensation as a *bonne bouche*. Aided by his profound studies in palæontology and embryology, he plunges, when discoursing of the eye, into those remote periods when eyes and vertebræ as yet were not, and Nature had only unfolded the first few leaves of her wondrous volume. During this description of the gradual evolution of the eye out of an infolded portion of the epidermis, by some such process of mutation as that which is held to have produced the rudiment of a spinal column, the attention of the audience is intense.

Adroitly concluding a lecture of absorbing interest with this astounding bit of speculative philosophy, Professor Huxley dismisses his audience before giving them time to recover breath. A few stroll about the Geological Museum, lighted up for the occasion, but the larger number, including the writer, march homewards, thoroughly charmed with a lecture which has given them something to weigh and think over in their leisure moments.

VII.

THE LONDON INSTITUTION.

To the present generation of Londoners few localities are less known than Finsbury Circus. Only a few short years ago, Finsbury altogether was very much a *terra incognita*. The existence of a square was dimly hinted at by foreign professors, who were supposed to affect that tranquil spot for residential purposes; the Circus was laid down in maps of the metropolis, but was seldom reached except by the festive members of the Honourable Artillery Company—whose stronghold is not far off—and a market where nobody ever went, and where nothing was ever bought or sold, enjoyed a place on the list of metropolitan commercial centres; but the entire district maintained but a dim and shadowy entity. Travellers into this silent region found their movements somewhat facilitated by the opening of the Metropolitan Railway, and easily attained thereby a point of departure for their wanderings, but the Moorgate Street Station has failed to infuse any vitality into the mysterious neighbourhood over the way. The main use of Finsbury has been to show to the adventurous spirits who penetrate into its recesses that there can be a duller place than Bloomsbury, and that the square of that ilk is the abode of bustling life and boisterous mirth, when contrasted with the dismal region of Finsbury.

Far away in the dim recesses of this sleeping—if not utterly dead and buried—city, on the dismallest side of the dismal Circus, is a huge building, founded for the best of all purposes, and called the London Institution. The gloom which weighs over the entire district sits heavily on this grim structure. Persons of a ribald turn of mind have long expressed a wish that a line of railway would carry away the entire affair, and lift it at once into the superior stratum of dead and gone institutions. Other irreverent beings have taken a fiendish delight in circulating reports of the existence of an enormous fungus destined at some period to lift the house up from its foundations. Nevertheless it looks solid enough and serious enough, and altogether a most unlikely building to perform any act of a saltatory nature.

Although the ceremony of laying the first stone of the London Institution was not performed until November 4th, 1815, on which occasion the speaker of the inaugural oration expressed a hope that the Gresham lectures—an equally lively institution—might find a home within its walls—it had been practically founded at a much earlier date. On October 17, 1805, a general meeting of proprietors was held, and laws and bye-laws agreed upon. In 1807 it was further consolidated by a Royal Charter of Incorporation. The number of proprietors was limited to one thousand, and the qualification of a proprietor was fixed at one hundred guineas—a privilege that at this moment may be secured by transfer for about one-tenth of that sum, and an annual payment of £2 due at Midsummer. In the year 1806 the groundwork of the library was laid by large purchases at the sale of the library of the Marquis of Lansdowne. Among the chief proprietors at this period were the late Sir Francis Baring, John Julius Angerstein—the collector of what is now the National Gallery—George Hibbert, and Richard Sharp. Nearly £80,000 had already been collected, and, pending the erection of the present building, the mansion erected by Sir Thomas Clayton in 1671 was first taken; but in 1811 the library was removed to King's Arms Yard, and a few years later to the present building. Few English libraries possess a finer collection of the historical and topographical literature of England than the London Institution

Foreign and general history are also amply supplied, and voyages and travels occupy a considerable space. Theology, law, and medicine are less fully represented, but in the mathematical sciences the library is very well furnished. A library over which Porson presided, if only for a brief period, should not be wanting in classics, and the London Institution possesses a noble series both in texts and in translations. Among the purchases and presents made to this collection are many of those choice specimens of early printing, which appeal more to the mere bibliograph than to the actual student. Here are the productions of Antonio Verard, the Wechels, the Stephani, the Aldi, the Sessi, and the Giunti, in addition to many choice specimens of early English printing. Great store is set by an "Orosius" without date or place of imprint, a complete series of folio Shakespeares, and a curious Chinese block book, entitled "Liber organicus Astronomiæ Europææ apud Sinas restitutæ," printed at Pekin in 1668. A collection of Spanish laws is highly prized from the use to which this copy was turned on the trial of Sir Thomas Picton for putting Luisa Calderon to the torture during his Governorship of Trinidad.

Between 1806 and 1812 the sum of £16,533 was expended on this library, and numerous additions have since been made. The reign of Richard Porson, from

1806 to 1808, though short, was not uneventful. Brilliant scholars are not invariably the best possible librarians, and it is recorded by Mr. Maltby, his successor, that the great Grecian received on one occasion a decided "wigging" from the Directors. The censure was conveyed in these very pointed terms, "We only know you are our librarian by seeing your name attached to the receipts for your salary." This vigorous reproof may, perhaps, have been merited, but certainly did not kill Porson, whose hide was proof against trifles of this kind.

The present number of volumes exceeds 62,000. The right of admission belongs exclusively to the proprietors. Each of these is provided with a transferable medal and card, thanks to which custom the few readers in the library present a juvenile appearance, which inclines the casual spectator to think that papa, being busy himself, has sent the boys round. Meanwhile the library, mainly on account of the difficulty of finding out proprietors, and the trouble of obtaining admittance, is practically abandoned by scholars, who far prefer the facilities afforded by the British Museum and the City Library at Guildhall. Originally founded to maintain, in what was once a central position, an extensive general library of reference, comprising works of intrinsic value and utility in all languages, reading-rooms for periodical publications, daily papers, and interesting contemporaneous pamphlets, and to promote the diffusion of knowledge by lecture and *conversazioni*, the London Institution started into life with objects sufficiently ambitious. But in addition to the fixed general library, a circulating library has been formed or the proprietors by subscriptions paid to Messrs. W. H. Smith and Son, and Rolandi's foreign library. This permanent circulating library has assumed proportions possibly undreamt of by its founders, inasmuch as it has eclipsed its rivals, the permanent library and the lectures, which latter—albeit occasionally delivered by men of celebrity in the world of science—have shrunk to very narrow proportions. Only two lectures are delivered per week—one at four p.m. on Mondays, and one at seven p.m. on Wednesdays.

In the synopsis for the past season, the two professors regularly attached to the institution—Professor Bentley (Botany) and Professor Armstrong (Chemistry)—were only down for two short courses of lectures. Professor Armstrong delivered a so-called Holiday Course on Oxygen and Carbon during the Christmas holidays, and then disappeared from the synopsis, while Professor Bentley's name was only down for half a dozen lectures on Elementary Botany. It is much to be regretted that the energies of Professor Armstrong should be confined to a few school-boy entertainments at Christmas-tide, and that Professor Bentley should be compelled to limit his efforts to six lectures on Elementary Botany. Poignancy is added to this reflection by the recollection that the London Institution has—as at present—often secured the services of distinguished scientific men as permanent professors. In the case of the chemistry lectures I need only mention the names of Professors Grove and Wanklyn to prove my position; but perhaps the reason for a paucity of lectures of a really practical educational character is that the remuneration given to the regular lecturers is very inadequate. At one time the chemical lecturer received fifty guineas per annum, supplemented by a like amount for expenses incurred in the laboratory and for experiments, but I hear with regret that the supplementary allowance has since been withdrawn, and that the chemical lectures, to which Dr. Armstrong could do ample justice, have been curtailed in consequence of this reduction. It is always depressing to find direct teaching set aside in favour of lectures on Art and Poetry, which, however agreeable and entertaining in the hands of Professors Zerffi and Morley, hardly supply the place of positive instruction. Art and Poetry are delightful subjects to talk about, write about, and listen to, but it is difficult to see how any human being could learn—by listening to any conceivable number of lectures—how to draw a figure from the solid, or how to write a smooth couplet. Music, poetry, and drawing are no more to be acquired by listening to lectures than the mystery of tight-rope dancing is to be learned by witnessing a performance of the accomplished Monsieur Blondin. My humble remarks on this question by no means apply to the more positive sciences, such as geometry, astronomy, geology, palæontolgy, and chemistry, all of which, especially the last-named, can—granted the faculty of lucid exposition on the part of the lecturer, and severe attention on the part of the student—be acquired to a very considerable extent by a rigid attendance at lectures, and, indeed, cannot be perfectly studied without the demonstration of a professor, while lectures on the three subjects previously mentioned can only be designated as "pleasant talk," conveying very little, if any, positive instruction to audience. Many philosophers incline to the view that there is in these latter days too much of this general talk, and, judging from what I witnessed at a lecture on the Development of Civilization, delivered one Monday afternoon by Dr. Tylor, I am inclined—until better instructed—to agree with the philosophers aforesaid.

The lecture theatre—spacious enough, but pervaded with a singularly earthy smell, as of a newly-opened vault—was occupied on the Monday afternoon in question by a miscellaneous crowd, wherein ladies of a tender age and small boys largely predominated. The lecture originally set down for the day, on "Magnetism and Current Electricity," had, possibly from causes beyond control, fallen through, and Dr. Tylor had obligingly filled up the gap with a discourse on the "Development of Civilization"—an exhilarating subject, but falling, unhappily, under the previously quoted designation of "talk about things." The lecturer held forth ably enough, and was at times, especially when he dwelt upon the influence of female opinion on savage communities—somewhat too noisily applauded.

He displayed considerable skill in the evolution of his theory of "animism," or the natural predilection of the savage to invest rivers, storms, stocks, and stones with a demoniac individuality, and at times made me tremble lest he should be induced to push his theory to the extreme limits which would, under similar circumstances, have been infallibly reached by my friend Professor Hohensziel, of the University of Ausbruch. The lecturer, however, kept on tolerably safe ground, albeit he startled his audience by maintaining that in rascality and general villainy the savage was not so far in advance of his civilized brother as is often imagined. All this was vastly entertaining and cheering to the souls of those who believe that depravity is not a very variable quantity, and that the ancient highwayman's place is now amply filled by the modern forger. But it was strong meat for babes. Not that in saying this do I intend to impute any fault to Dr. Tylor. Far from it. If the management of the London Institution choose to admit what I am afraid I must call "a parcel of children" to lectures supposed to interest mature, or nearly mature, human beings, no fault can be laid at the door of the lecturer. If, however, that learned gentleman—who is full of ideas—had chosen to write out his lecture fairly before reading it, I should have been happier, inasmuch as I should have been spared the pain of hearing him strive painfully to weave his notes into coherent and concatenated sentences. Nevertheless, the lecturer exhibited great research and a judicious choice of illustrations, coupled with a power of generalization which compelled me to regret that it had not been my good fortune to hear his discourse in the finished form of a *concio ad clerum*.

Unfortunately it is difficult to resist the conclusion that, in lectures of a presumedly popular kind, the high priest is, either from a desire to court popularity or from a good-natured contempt for his audience, but too often inclined to talk down to their level, and thereby produce in many listeners the conviction that a good thing has been marred by an ineffectual endeavour to adapt it to the assumed mental capacity —or incapacity—of the listener. I am irresistibly impelled to lift up my voice and cry, "In heaven's name let us have one thing or the other." On the one hand, let us have lectures purely educational, which, beginning from first principles, teach the young idea to seize upon elementary truths, to grasp them firmly, and to advance by degrees to an accurate conception of great problems or great ascertained facts. On the other hand, let us now and then, at least, hear a lecture which takes a certain amount of knowledge for granted, and tells the already educated men and women of the world something they want to know, without descending to minute particulars, small jokes, or homely illustrations. With a few great exceptions the style of lecturing now in vogue is abominable. It is neither one thing nor the other, and lecturers, in the vain endeavour to arrest the attention of uneducated persons, stoop to meretricious arts which weary when they do not irritate those among their audience who, on other subjects, are as well instructed as themselves.

Truth to tell, I leave the London Institution a prey to a feeling of depression. The huge lecture theatre half full of women and children, and the rich library barren of scholars, and only invaded by boys coming to change novels at the circulating department, afflict me with sore reflections on the vanity of many human, and especially London, institutions. What is the outcome of eighty thousand pounds? A gloomy building, a couple of underpaid professors, and a like number of sub-librarians overworked in changing books for children, a few "popular" lectures, a squadron of discontented shareholders, and an autocratic hall-porter.

VIII.

THE BIRKBECK INSTITUTE.

In the mysterious locality known as "round the corner," the Birkbeck Institution enjoys a vigorous existence. Shrinking back from the rush and roar of Holborn into the quietest nook of Southampton Buildings, this busy hive of literary and scientific bees is hardly so well known by its new title as under its original designation of the London Mechanics' Institution. This, the parent of many hundreds of similar institutions scattered over the whole length and breadth of the country, owed its foundation mainly to the public spirit and liberality of the distinguished scientific man whose name it now bears, and in whose mind the idea of founding an institution for the instruction of artisans was developed by the following events. During his residence in Glasgow, about the commencement of the present century, Dr. George Birkbeck, needing various scientific instruments and apparatus for the lectures he was delivering at the Andersonian University, found himself embarrassed by the impossibility of finding in Glasgow any competent person to whom he could entrust the work. Nothing daunted, Dr. Birkbeck determined to attend the different workshops himself, and to personally direct the construction of the apparatus he required. Greatly impressed by the intelligence displayed by the artisans with whom he was thus brought into contact, and interested by their constant inquiries for the reason of various steps in the work, he became convinced of the absolute necessity for affording scientific instruction to skilled workmen, and therefore resolved to commence a course of gratuitous lectures, and to form special classes for instructing the artisans of Glasgow in the various branches of Natural Philosophy. The first lecture was delivered to an audience of seventy-five, the second was attended by nearly two hundred, the third by three hundred, while at the fourth five hundred artisans availed themselves of the opportunity of obtaining instruction calculated to assist them in their daily employment. So sudden and eager was the appreciation by the Glasgow workmen of the value of the teaching generously offered to them that it became necessary to restrict the issue of tickets, and so satisfied was Dr. Birkbeck with the success of his experiment that he continued to give these lectures for several years, until his removal to London.

On settling in the metropolis Dr. Birkbeck, although actively engaged in his profession, entered heartily into a scheme for the erection of an institution which, by lectures, classes, a reading-room, and a library, should spread literary, scientific, and artistic instruction among the artisans of London. At the present day, when education is more talked about than anything else, a movement of this kind would appear simple and natural enough; but it must be recollected that these events occurred more than fifty years ago, and that too much honour cannot be rendered to him who was the heart and soul of the first great effort in this country to extend to artisans the benefit of that higher education which, until then, had been restricted to the more wealthy classes.

Public meetings were called on the 11th November and on the 2nd December, 1823, and several hundreds enrolled their names as members of the proposed institution. Dr. Birkbeck was unanimously chosen president, and continued to hold that post till his decease on the 2nd December, 1841, on the eighteenth anniversary of the establishment of the Institution. By the death of its revered president and founder the London Mechanics' Institution suffered a loss which at the time was felt to be irreparable. His unvarying kindness to the members and his great interest in their welfare had endeared him to their memory, and their gratitude for his noble work is to be seen in the handsome medallion by the late Mr. Foley, which surmounts the platform of the lecture theatre. The public appreciation of the labours of Dr. Birkbeck was shown by the foundation by public subscription of the "Birkbeck Laboratory" at University College. On the death of the founder the office of president was by the unanimous wish of the members bestowed on his son, Mr. W. Lloyd Birkbeck, who has ever since rivalled his distinguished father in devotion to the interests of the Institution.

In his great work Dr. Birkbeck was zealously supported by the late Duke of Sussex, the Duke of Bedford, the Marquis of Lansdowne, Lord Althorp, Lord Brougham, Sir Francis Burdett, and many other noblemen and gentlemen distinguished for their scientific and literary attainments. The late Lord—then Mr. Henry—Brougham, took especial interest in the institution, and, amid his multifarious occupations, found time to put in a frequent appearance at the lectures, setting a valuable example to others by his own deep attention. Launched under favourable auspices, the institution was not only a success in itself, but formed a model for all similar establishments. Temples of science sprang up all over the country, until at the present moment there is hardly a town of any importance in the United Kingdom which is not possessed of its literary or mechanics' institution. The colonies also have followed the example of the mother country by founding hundreds of organizations modelled upon the parent institution in Southampton Buildings.

The work achieved by the London Mechanics' Institution has been neither slight nor insignificant. During the forty-nine years following its foundation, fifty thousand persons availed themselves of its advantages, and many of these have found the education received under these circumstances the stepping-stone to distinguished position. Every branch of art, science, and literature has been recruited from students trained at Southampton Buildings, and owing to the valuable aid afforded by the examinations of the Society of Arts and of the Science and Art Department, the practical and immediate value of the instruction afforded has been greatly increased. During an existence extending over half a century there have been times when the success of the Institution was less conspicuous than at others, but since the recent impetus given to education and the application to the Institution of the name of its founder, a great advance has been made. The number of students exceeds two thousand seven hundred, a result to which the unremitting labour of Mr. George M. Norris, the manager and honorary secretary of the Educational Council, has contributed in no slight degree.

This Educational Council is a noteworthy body, inasmuch as it presides over and directly manages the educational working of the Institution. Composed partly of well-known and practical sympathizers with working-class education, and partly of teachers in the Institution, who necessarily have a deep insight into the needs and feelings of the students, the Council is keenly aware of the wants and aspirations of the great body of members. A feeling is also growing that, so far as is possible, teachers and members of the Council should be drawn from the ranks of successful scholars, with a view of knitting together still more closely those kindly relations which should always exist between teachers and pupils.

The terms on which instruction is imparted are exceedingly moderate. An annual subscription of eighteen shillings, dating from the day of payment, secures a free admission to the weekly lectures, entertainments, and reading-room, and the free use of a library of 7000 volumes. Another privilege conferred by membership is admission to special classes at about half the price charged to the general public. For instance, French is charged *5s.* per term to the general public, and 3*s*. to members; and experimental physics, 7*s*. 6*d*. to the public, and 3*s*. to members. For like infinitesimal sums instruction may be had in about fifty subjects, "to enumerate which would," as the old saw hath it, "be long." Suffice it to say that teaching may be had in mathematics, including geometry (plane and solid), trigonometry (plane and spherical), the differential and integral calculus, the calculus of finite differences, actuarial computations, navigation, and geometrical conics ; and in applied and theoretical mechanics—by members for nothing—and by the public for 3*s*. per session, it having been wisely concluded that instruction in these positive branches of knowledge should be granted on the lowest possible terms.

A perusal of the last report of the Educational Council is highly interesting as affording an index of the comparative popularity of the numerous classes now in actual work. An inspection of this document leads to the conclusion that the muscular young gentleman once depicted in *Punch*, in the act of observing to a delicate-looking child, "I can't play the piano, and I can't speak French; but I can punch your head," was very much behind the spirit of the age. No less than 450 students attended the French classes, while 727 joined the various music and singing classes. As an attractive language, German comes next to

French, with 177 students; Latin follows *magno intervallo;* after which come Spanish, Italian, and Greek in the order named. The English language, literature, grammar, and composition secure but 205 names, while elocution draws 124. The mathematical and arithmetical classes are well attended, as are also the classes for experimental physics, chemistry, and mechanics. Geometrical, model, and ornamental drawing, perspective, building and machine construction, figure and landscape drawing, are popular subjects; as are also shorthand, writing, and physiology. It is, perhaps, a little disappointing to find the number of students of "fancy" subjects exceed so largely that of those pursuing the severer branches of knowledge; but it must not be forgotten that lady scholars are admitted to the Birkbeck Institution, and that the demand for musical instruction is in a considerable degree referrible to this fact. Moreover, a certain amount of consolation may be found in the numbers attending the French and German classes. In no department of knowledge have Englishmen hitherto been so deficient as in modern languages. Many middle-aged Englishmen find it impossible to pronounce a French word in recognizable fashion, and it would not be difficult to find wranglers and first-class men who, albeit loaded to the muzzle with Greek, Latin, and mathematics, find it impossible to string together half a dozen intelligible French sentences. This, however, like other insular defects, will doubtless be cured in time.

Wending my way towards the "Birkbeck," on a fine bright evening, I confess within myself certain doubts as to where it is. A walk along Holborn, however, brings me to Southampton Buildings, and a turn "round the corner" to the institution itself. The ground floor is occupied by the Birkbeck Bank, and this arrangement considerably reduces the small space available for the institution. Cheered by the sound of distant music, I make my way into the great lecture theatre, a structure so ample and commodious as to still further crowd the narrow class-rooms. Here I find a singing class in full operation, under the care of a teacher, who displays much patience and more energy in getting his class of some three hundred persons to sing in tune, and keep together. The sight is agreeable enough. Well-dressed young ladies and smart young men occupy the benches, and exercise their lungs vigorously, but I am a little disappointed at finding among them no trace of the artisan or his helpmate, and come reluctantly to the conclusion that either workmen have taken to dress very elegantly, or that the singing class is mainly composed of clerks and young ladies in similar positions of life. A little dashed at this, I pull myself together for something serious, and ask my way to the chemistry class, and after travelling over many stairs find myself in an apartment which, were it not consecrated to the uses of science, I should not hesitate to designate the back kitchen. Bare white-washed walls throw up the inevitable black board into strong relief, and a couple of flaring "butchers' lights" illumine a rough deal table, from behind which Mr. Chaloner lucidly expounds the properties of carbonic acid gas. The lecturer and the audience evidently mean business. The students are mostly pale young men—reminding me of the traditional "pale student" who bent over the "midnight oil" *Consule Planco*—a personage entirely out of fashion since the invention of muscular Christianity, and the growth of a pretty general belief that, although a senior wrangler may be a deserving young man, the stroke oar of the winning eight over the Putney course is a hero. Older men, however, are not absent, and all are busily engaged in taking notes, evidently with a view to standing fire at the next "exam."

This, now, is refreshing. Here, in this crowded back-kitchen, honest work is evidently being done. But the visitor may not dwell longer even upon carbonic acid gas, and makes his way up a staircase to a reading-room, crowded to an inconvenient degree. Here are young and old, perusing books and periodicals, taking notes, making no noise, and reducing themselves to the smallest possible compass. The library is full of applicants awaiting their turn, and I become convinced that an atmosphere of bustle pervades the entire institution. Knowledge is sold here at a moderate price, the business is brisk, and the customers many.

On paying a second visit to the Birkbeck Institute, I find the mathematical class hard at work, the master appearing to be on the best terms with his pupils, who are working with a will. At this I am not surprised, as no human being would care to trifle or dally with algebra—mere *dilettanti* students almost invariably selecting some easier subject. Hardly so severe is the attention given to Mr. Wilson's lecture on optics, whereat many ladies are present. Sitting and listening, or mayhap, taking a few notes, put by no means so severe a strain upon the scholar as actual computation. It is possible for reasonable human beings to listen to lectures on physics and enjoy themselves very much, and this appears to be the case with the present class. Forsaking the lecturer, just as he is proving to his audience—experimentally—that the angle of reflection is equal to the angle of incidence, I mount more stairs and assist at an animated scene. The elocution class is in full blast, and perhaps combines more amusement with instruction than any class I ever attended. The master is perspiring with his exertions in endeavouring to inspire the scholars with some of that energy of which he possesses an ample share. I do not—on mature reflection—think that I should like to be a teacher of elocution. This valuable pursuit may, like other professions, have its peculiar consolations and subtle pleasures, but to the uninitiated it seems but dull work, this striving to inoculate the untutored mind with some little taste and accuracy in speaking or reading a plain sentence. Nevertheless, elocution is a good thing, if only for its use in teaching some little respect for the letter *h*, a hapless aspirate utterly disregarded by thorough-bred Londoners. Only those who discourse daily with all sorts and conditions of men are in a condition to explain their annoyance at being compelled to listen to the absurdly vulgar Cockney dialect. It absolutely flays "ears polite," which could listen with comparative pleasure to a rasping "burr" or a "brogue thick enough to cut with a knife." A distinguished Frenchman once remarked that in England two distinct languages are spoken: one strongly accentuated and almost painfully distinct—the language of the highly-educated class—and the other, slurred, confused, and mumbled, so as to be almost unintelligible. So by all means let us have elocution, and as much of it as possible.

Coming downstairs again I step into another cell in this knowledge-hive, and find a botany class in progress, but my time is getting short, and I am compelled to descend once more into the depths, where a large drawing class is hard at it. In a semi-circular cavern, hung round with plaster casts, and lighted with flaring gas, is crowded together a large number of pupils busy over their drawing boards, and applying themselves to their work with the persistence generally observed in those who pay for their instruction out of their own hardly-earned wages. There is no dawdling and no "larking" visible, and the spirit of work which apparently inspires every department of the "Birkbeck" is clearly dominant in this ill-lighted cellar, where, in spite of every disadvantage, valuable knowledge and technical dexterity can be acquired by those who seek for them.

Stepping at length from the heated atmosphere of the busy "Birkbeck" into the cool evening air, I cannot help reflecting on my visit with considerable pleasure. Here is an institution entirely self-supporting, unaided by subventions of any kind. It sells knowledge and good sound practical, technical teaching at a fabulously low price, and yet maintains itself in a solvent condition without assistance from those grumbling shareholders, who sit like an incubus on more than one institution, and groan over the daily depreciation of their property. Cooped up in a narrow space, crowded nightly from garret to cellar, the Birkbeck Institute is well enough managed to get through an immense amount of good honest useful work. It is in every respect an important aid to education, and is invaluable to those classes which avail themselves of it; but, alas!—the inevitable *amari aliquid*—I should like to have seen a little more of the genuine mechanic.

IX.

THE GRESHAM LECTURES.

HAPPENING to pass along Basinghall Street, I was attracted by a programme setting forth the Gresham Lectures to be delivered during Hilary Term, 1874, in the lecture theatre of the building known as Gresham College. Seven subjects were to be discoursed upon:—Astronomy, Physic, Rhetoric, Law, Geometry, Divinity, and Music. The Latin lectures were to be delivered at six o'clock in the evening, and the English lectures at seven. The public were to be admitted gratis.

I had often heard of the Gresham Lectures, and had been frequently told by troublesome people, who are always worrying about progress and the nineteenth century and similar positive subjects, that the outcome of Sir Thomas Gresham's bequest had been very small indeed, and that great difficulty had been experienced at various times in getting anything done at all. Little more than a century and a quarter after the death of the worthy Knight in 1579, it was found necessary to draw attention to the management, or rather mismanagement, of Gresham College, in a pamphlet entitled, "An Account of the Rise, Foundation, Progress, and present State of Gresham College in London, with the Life of the Founder, Sir Thomas Gresham; as also of some late endeavours for obtaining the Revival and Restitution of the Lectures there, with some remarks thereon." This curious production, after setting forth the terms of Sir Thomas Gresham's will, complains bitterly that the provisions of the trust were not complied with, the number of lectures having been very much reduced from that prescribed by the will. The anonymous writer is inclined to attribute the disuse of the lectures to "the late troubles"—as convenient an explanation of everything in the seventeenth century, as was the French Revolution of everything in the nineteenth. Nevertheless, positive evidence exists that, during the protectorate of Cromwell, the attention of that great man was keenly pointed towards the Gresham professorships. In a letter preserved in the City Library at Guildhall, the great Puritan intervenes actively in the management of an election. This document is dated from Whitehall, 9th May, 1656, and is addressed to the Gresham Committee of the City of London, as follows:—"Gentlemen,—Wee understanding that you have appointed an election this afternoon of a geometry professor in Gresham Collidge, wee desire you to suspend the same for some tyme till we shall have an opportunitie to speak with you in order to that business.—Your louving friend, OLIVER P." From this document, it may safely be inferred that the Lord Protector looked sharply enough after the Gresham Committee. At what was called "the Happy Restauration of King Charles the Second," Gresham College was stirred into unusual activity by the Royal Society. Dr. Robert Hooke was at that time Professor of Geometry in Gresham College, and acquired so great a reputation as to induce Sir John Cutler to found a Mechanic Lecture. The Chair of Geometry was also filled by Isaac Barrow, and that of Astronomy by Sir Christopher Wren. Nevertheless, so great was the cause of complaint in 1706, that a memorial was laid before the Lord Mayor and the Court of Aldermen, setting forth that the subscribers had attended the lectures founded by Sir Thomas Gresham at Gresham College, which were devised by his will to be read "*every day in the week*, for the Instruction of Youth and others of this city in useful knowledge. But the present professors read *only in Term Time*," etc. The writer of the pamphlet, moreover, avers that, although the greatest part of the professors "appear to be Gentlemen of Civility, Ingenuity, and Candour, yet they seemed to discover an unwillingness and reluctancy to perform so useful a work, because it required some pains and attendance, and were so far from the ambition of being crowded with auditors, that they seemed rather to desire to have none at all; for though they could not altogether disown their obligation to read the aforesaid lectures (without which acknowledgment they could not be entitled to their salaries), yet they pretended (without the least shadow of authority) to confine themselves to do it only in the Terms, and at those times, to render them more insignificant, they retrenched the first and last weeks of every Term." It also appears that the lecturers, "not content herewith, exempted themselves from the duty every holiday that happened in each Term, refusing to read on such a day, even though it were Divinity, by this means they reduced it to what was next to nothing; and together with the affronts of some on those that come to demand their lectures, the uncertainty of the times and days when they were to be read, the meanness and indifferency of some of them when they did read, being often without method, design, or regular handling a Subject, not confining themselves to their proper province but passing in a desultory manner from one subject to another, without that order and connection as might have been wished, so far discouraged and baulked the expectation of the auditory that they almost gained their point," and were very near being abandoned to their own devices and allowed to draw their salary without doing anything for it at all. Whether the Grand Committee for managing the affairs of Gresham College, which consisted then as now of four aldermen and eight commoners of the City of London and twelve commoners for the Company of Mercers, ever did anything in the matter is not very clear. Things went on more or less lamely in Gresham College—actually the mansion originally inhabited by Sir Thomas Gresham himself, extending from Bishopsgate Street to Broad Street, and which, on escaping from the Great Fire of London, became the Chamber, the Guildhall, the Common Hall, and the Exchange, of the remaining City. On this occasion the lodgings of the Divinity Professor were given up to the Lord Mayor, the reading-rooms were appropriated to the City courts and officers, the quadrangle was allotted to the merchants for an Exchange, and small shops were allowed to be built in the galleries and the piazza, for the accommodation of the poor tradesmen who had been burnt out of their shops at the Royal Exchange. "Thus Gresham College became an epitome of this great city, and the centre of all affairs, both public and private, which were then transacted in it."

In 1768, the College having fallen into a dilapidated

condition, and the Excise Office in the Old Jewry being also in a tumble-down state, the site of Gresham College was selected for the new Excise Office. True reverence for antique monuments was not a characteristic of the latter half of the eighteenth century. The site and buildings were alienated to the Crown on payment to the City and Mercers Company of a perpetual rent of £500 per annum; the City and Company paying £1800 down towards the expense of pulling down the College and erecting the new office. On this occasion "the collegiate establishment was entirely subverted." In lieu of a college with resident celibate professors, a room at the Royal Exchange was set apart for reading the lectures, and the professors were allowed £50 a year in lieu of apartments, over and above the original salary of £50 a year for reading the lectures. The evil effect of this total reversal of the condition enjoined by the will of Sir Thomas Gresham was soon made manifest. The lectures were scantily attended, partly owing to the inconvenient hour at which they were held, and partly owing to the advanced age of many of the lecturers, a natural consequence of residence and celibacy being dispensed with. The average number of the audience at the lectures, from 1800 to 1820 inclusive, was only ten per English lecture, and thirteen at all the Latin lectures for the whole year.

After the burning of the Royal Exchange the Gresham Lectures enjoyed a nomadic existence until 1841, when the Joint Gresham Committee purchased a plot of ground at the corner of Basinghall Street and Gresham Street, and erected on it the present building, at a cost of £7000. This was opened on the 2nd of November, 1843.

From time to time slight modifications have been introduced into the Gresham Lectures, with a view to making them of some intelligible use. After a prolonged struggle the professors were brought to issue a syllabus of lectures, and as the old hands were slowly gathered to their fathers the hours of lecturing were transferred to the evening, and things were said to be much better managed.

Still, uncomfortable rumours had reached me and had excited my curiosity. It was reported that persons had vainly striven to obtain admission to the Latin lectures; that the doors were only opened for five minutes just before six o'clock, and were then summarily closed unless within that short space of time three persons had obtained entrance—no smaller number being considered an audience. It was openly declared that by a careful observance of these precautions the professors, who received £100 per annum for reading at most twelve Latin and twelve English lectures, generally contrived to evade the Latin lecture altogether. At any rate, I failed to unearth any human being who had ever heard a Gresham lecture, and was thereupon moved to make an excursion in search of information conveyed in the vehicle of an ancient language.

Finding announced for the evening of Friday, the 23rd of January, a lecture on Geometry, by the Very Reverend B. M. Cowie, B.D., Dean of Manchester, I presented myself at Gresham College at five minutes before six. Possibly all people look mean when in search of information; at any rate, I have no doubt I did; for on slinking into the hall-way I received from a remarkably fine specimen of the British beadle a glance wherein astonishment and contempt were deliciously blended. Escaping as quickly as possible from the awful presence of this magnate, I found myself the solitary tenant of a huge lecture-room, garnished with particularly hard and uncomfortable seats of that peculiar make which is supposed to conduce to the preservation of a vigilant attitude. Fervently hoping that two more victims would turn up before the clock struck six, I sat down on one of the benches, hard as the nether millstone, and glanced around me in tranquil wretchedness.

The lecture theatre presented a dreary aspect. A dim religious light revealed the dismal scene. A peculiar atmosphere—suggestive of long-since departed lecturers and of audiences gone ages since to their rest—pervaded the hall of despair. In the absence of living, breathing human beings, it was not difficult for the imagination to conjure up visions of departed worthies. Seated gravely in the midst appeared the form of Sir Thomas Gresham himself, surrounded by a crowd of knights and scholars clad in doublet, trunk hose, and agonizing ruffs, or in the velvet gowns proper to great merchants and citizens of the chief city of the State. The thoughful yet eager and enthusiastic Raleigh, yet young, was holding solemn converse with the great merchant, and evidently trying to impress him with the certain success of the Great Eldorado Company, Limited. Lilly and the hero of Zutphen were there, giving a courtly air to the proceedings; while in a remote corner sat "rare Ben Jonson," poet, wit, and scholar, deprecating in his heart of hearts the utilitarian tendency of the age, and foreseeing, in the passion for enterprise and greed of gain that had suddenly overcome the nation, a parallel condition of things to that which prevailed in Rome before the smouldering conspiracy of Catiline burst into the flames of civil war.

Harvey, still young, with pale, worn face, deep in thought, not having yet lighted on his grand discovery of the circulation of the blood, anxiously awaited the commencement of the lecture, while a choice knot of navigators—Cavendish and Frobisher, Drake, and bluff Sir John Hawkins—surrounded by a few of the old crew of that tall ship, the *Pelican*, discoursed largely on the state of affairs in the Spanish main and the golden sands of remote California. A slight bustle at the door, and in troops a merry crowd of dramatists full of glee, warmed by the generous wine dispensed at that famous hostelry, the "Mermaid." But the clock strikes six, and at that sound the weird spectres vanish, and I become aware that I am not living in the age of Armadas, Manilla galleons, inquisitions, and St. Bartholomew massacres, but am sitting on a hard wooden bench, in what is now merely the core of the modern Babylon, and that the date is January 23rd, 1874.

Looking around in search of an audience I make out, with some difficulty, a total of seven persons, all of the male sex. Two of these cautiously remain near the door, as if uncertain as to the duration of their sojourn, while the remaining five—adventurous spirits these—boldly occupy the body of the theatre. No gorgeous doublets or stupendous ruffs adorn the persons of these visitors, the place of those articles of raiment being supplied by seedy overcoats and limp shirt-collars—serrated as to their edges. Swords they wear none—well-worn umbrellas of sober alpaca, or modest gingham, assimilating better with the sad-coloured raiment of the nineteenth century. These men are clearly not youthful students, but, for all that, take no small interest in the proceedings—especially one slender gentleman with a studious cast of features. Another and smaller gentleman with a beard takes notes vigorously, while a burly, bull-necked man struggles desperately to invest his features with a look of attentive intelligence.

Ushered in by the superb beadle, the lecturer—a bright, pleasant-looking gentleman (by the way, not the Dean of Manchester, who probably has other and bigger fish to fry elsewhere)—puts in appearance. At first I am inclined to sympathize with this victim to empty benches, but on reflecting that he probably clears some four or five guineas by the transaction, I restrain my feelings, which, moreover, undergo singular changes as the evening advances—alternating between calm endurance, nervous irritability, savage fury, and stolid despair.

Advancing to the table, and casting a glance of patient resignation at the meagre audience, the lecturer proceeds *maximâ celeritate* to—as the French call it—"execute himself." He is supplied with a manuscript well-thumbed and worn, and exhibiting a marked tendency to dogs' ears. Away he dashes at a tearing pace, as if determined to make short work of the lecture—a singular Latin disquisition written with very little regard to classic grace, albeit abundantly seasoned with lengthy Greek quotations clumsily strung together like pearls on rotten twine. The lecture is carried on almost entirely in the language of Plato and Aristotle, who are laid heavily under contribution. Diogenes Laertius is also heavily drawn upon, and the entire composition assumes the appearance of a burlesque on one of those mediæval disquisitions wherein profuse quotation is made to supply the place of original thought. The third Greek quotation makes short work of the man nearest the door, who, evidently recollecting an engagement, beats a hasty retreat. His neighbour exhibits greater powers of endurance, and fights bravely against a crushing sense of fatigue till a huge slab of Diogenes Laertius finally demolishes him, and he retires precipitately a sadder, if not a wiser man. Shortly after this the central phalanx shows signs of disintegration—a quiet gentleman, who had up to this point struggled manfully against a propensity to yawn, being finally killed off by a highly interesting and absorbing investigation into the question whether Thales did or did not import geometry from Egypt into Greece. The listeners are now reduced to four, evidently determined to be in at the death; but the most stalwart these of clearly wishes himself away, and is only restrained from executing a flank movement by a feeling of courtesy towards the lecturer, who still reads on at a rapid pace. Calm despair at length takes possession of the audience, whose countenances indicate four distinct shades of misery when the lecturer, after a rapid rush of words, arrives at the final *dixi*. Before forsaking the gloomy scene this gentleman addresses a few courteous sentences to the audience, deprecating any severe criticism of the Latin lecture. It was invariably so thinly attended, and so frequently not attended at all, that it had been thought unnecessary to devote any particular attention to the writing of the Latin lecture, but if better and more appreciative audiences could be counted upon, better Latin lectures would have been prepared. Moreover, an English lecture on trigonometry would be delivered at seven o'clock, and perhaps might prove more intelligible to an audience presumably unable to understand Latin. This is all vastly well, of course, but I fail to see why —if a Latin lecture must be delivered—it should not be a good one; nor is it sun clear why a Latin lecture should consist almost entirely of Greek quotations, and be confined exclusively to the history of ancient geometry. Does a mysterious glamour come over English scholars when they undertake the task of Latin prose composition? Do they feel themselves compelled to ignore all allusion to discoveries in mathematical science by the moderns, who, whatever their inferiority to the ancients in other respects, are certainly not behind them in scientific acquirements? Is it felt that anything less than a couple of thousand years old should not be written of in Latin, or is the whole dreary performance recognized by writers of Latin discourses, as a ridiculous anachronism? If so, they agree with the scanty audience, *quorum pars magna fui*, and the sooner the whole sham is abolished the better.

An interval of a quarter of an hour suffices to recuperate my energies sufficiently for the English lecture. The theatre at seven o'clock is, as compared with its condition at six, absolutely crowded. Nearly forty persons must be present, and among them are several ladies. The lecture lasts an hour, and is in many respects a curious production, conveying the idea that an attempt is being made to teach trigonometry to persons entirely ignorant of even the first book of Euclid. This difficulty hampers the lecturer sadly, and in the endeavour to grapple with it much time is cut to waste. To begin with, the fourth proposition of the first book requires a lengthy exposition. A knowledge of the proposition that if in any two triangles, two sides of similar length enclose similar angles, the third sides shall also be equal each to each, and enclose similar angles—although indispensable as a stepping-stone to the *pons asinorum*, and necessary to a proper comprehension of trigonometry —might surely be assumed in a lecture on the latter science.

An acquaintance with the nature of a right-angled triangle, and the division of the circumference of a circle into 360 degs., might also, I should think, be safely assumed in persons ambitious to acquire the useful science of trigonometry.

By a desire to teach this pretty branch of mathematics without pre-supposing the slightest mathematical knowledge, the lecturer constantly finds his progress arrested by the necessity for recurring to the primary truths of geometry. The effort is laudable because well meant, but can hardly prove either interesting or instructive to any class of auditors. Those ignorant of the first book of Euclid can hardly be taught the propositions necessary to a comprehension of trigonometry within the limits of a lecture, while those to whom elementary mathematics are familiar, are simply tired and bored to death by twice-told tales. The whole attempt is just like trying to teach children to read without making them learn their A B C. Thanks to recent improvements in the method of teaching mathematics, Euclid has been made easy to minds of the slenderest capacity. There is thus no excuse for those who, wishing to take a short cut to trigonometry, find it, without a slight acquaintance with geometry and algebra, the longest way round.

It is disappointing to find that, in an age when so much talk is heard about education, no better employment can be found for the Gresham bequests than in lectures from which no human being can possibly learn anything. Lectures may either be addressed to students who are supposed to know something, or to the public who may—if it please the lecturer—be supposed to know nothing; but Latin lectures on the purely historical aspect of a science, and English lectures which profess—if they profess anything—to teach trigonometry to persons totally ignorant of the first principles of mathematics, can only be regarded as anachronisms and blunders. The *concio ad clerum* is simply ridiculous—the *concio ad populum* utterly impracticable and useless.

X.

THE SOCIETY OF TELEGRAPH ENGINEERS.

Springing from the recesses of the human mind at the period of that great upheaval of intelligence known as the "Renaissance," the stream of scientific knowledge—like a mountain torrent newly issued from its parent glacier—for a while progressed by leaps and bounds—diverted hither and thither by the rocks of superstition and scholasticism, and bore with it the opaque particles of tradition. Acquiring strength in its progress, the turbid flood by degrees assumed the proportions of a majestic river, which having undergone purification by its passage through the lake of Time, emerges at length comparatively bright and pure only to undergo subdivision into a myriad of minute rills, narrow indeed, but clear and well defined. Nature-knowledge, once comprised under the heads of alchemy and of astrology, has given birth to almost innumerable subdivisions of scientific thought. Forces once undreamt of have one by one been revealed to the patient investigator. The powers of steam, of water, and of electricity have by turns occupied the attention of the scientific world, and their practical application to the wants of mankind has engaged the energies of the engineer. For a while this great artificer of modern times essayed to hold in one hand and in one brain the art of making nature the handmaid of man; but the rapid development of scientific discovery and the exactions of modern life have, within our day, now compelled engineers—like other men of science—to devote themselves exclusively to one groove of their profession. Thus we now have the hydraulic, the railway, the mechanical, the mining, and lastly, the telegraph engineer.

Electric telegraphy, now second in importance to none of the great inventions which have given this country a practical character peculiarly its own, is, in simple English, a thing of yesterday. It is true that many of the properties of electricity had long been known, but the earliest discovery that it was possible to transmit electricity through considerable distances was made in 1727 by Stephen Gray, the first Copley medallist of the Royal Society, and afterwards—a pensioner of the Charter House! Various electricians repeated and improved upon his experiments, but the idea of transmitting intelligence by electricity was slowly evolved. The first person upon whom it dawned appears to have been Charles Marshall, who wrote a letter signed "C. M.," in the *Scots Magazine*, of the 1st of February, 1758, describing a perfectly practical system of electric telegraphy which could, if better systems were not in operation, be advantageously used at the present day. At the period just referred to, frictional electricity, the kind least adapted for telegraphic purposes, was the only electricity known. Owing to this and other reasons, the electric telegraph remained for a long time in an embryonic state, albeit the late Sir Francis Ronalds, prior to 1816, made many interesting experiments, and ultimately erected a complete electric telegraph on his lawn at Hammersmith. In his endeavours to obtain recognition of his invention by the Government of the day, he was not more fortunate than the inventor who propounded a somewhat similar scheme to Napoleon. He received, in reply to his note pressing the electric telegraph upon the notice of the Admiralty, the following thoroughly official letter from Mr., afterwards Sir John, Barrow: —

"Mr. Barrow presents his compliments to Mr. Ronalds, and acquaints him, with reference to his note of the 3rd inst., that telegraphs of any kind are now wholly unnecessary, and that no other than the one now in use will be adopted."

Sir Francis Ronalds was not a man to be disheartened by an official rebuff, and pursuing his experiments, published in 1823 his "Description of an Electrical Telegraph," in which occurs the following prophetic passage: —

"Why has no serious trial yet been made of the qualifications of so diligent a courier? And if it should be proved competent to the task, why should not our kings hold councils at Brighton, with their ministers in London? Why should not our Government govern at Portsmouth almost as promptly as in Downing Street? Why should our defaulters escape by default of our foggy climate? And since our piteous *inamorati* are not all Alphei, why should they add to the torments of absence those dilatory tormentors, pens, ink, paper, and posts? Let us have electrical conversazione offices, communicating with each other, all over the kingdom, if we can."

Meanwhile an immense advance in electrical science was made by Œrsted, who in 1819 discovered that a magnetic needle could be moved by an electric current. On this principle—on Sturgeon's discovery that a piece of iron surrounded by electric currents becomes a magnet, and on the discovery by Sir Humphry Davy and others of the chemical decomposition occasioned by electrical currents—depends the modern science of telegraphy. An important contribution was also made in 1827 by Professor Ohm, who determined the laws which govern the passage of electric currents through conductors. Electricians, now able to move needles, to attract armatures, and to produce telegraphic signs on chemically-prepared paper, made a vast number of experiments. Perhaps the nearest approach to a practical application of newly-discovered powers was made by Baron Schilling in 1832, and by Steinheil in 1837. About this latter date the feasibility of electric telegraphy was not only admitted, but largely commented on in scientific lectures.

Many independent investigators were at work, and the usual race took place for the prize of praise or profit awarded to the first adaptation of principles to necessities. In the case of the electric telegraph, as in that of railways, the prize was destined to fall to England. In March, 1836, the present Sir William Fothergill Cooke was studying anatomy at Heidelberg, and, on attending Monck's Experimental Lectures on Physics, was so much struck with the power of electricity, and its obvious applicability to telegraphic purposes, that he relinquished his former pursuits and devoted his entire energies to the production of an electric telegraph. Returning at once to England, he made the acquaintance of John Lewis Ricardo, Robert

Stephenson, George Parker Bidder, and other wealthy and enterprising men, and laid his ideas before them. In February, 1837, he obtained an introduction to Sir Charles Wheatstone, who had attracted great attention by the lectures which he had previously delivered at King's College, and whose brilliant demonstration of the extreme velocity of electricity had astonished and delighted the scientific world. The meeting of Cooke and Wheatstone was destined to have a most important influence on the progress of telegraphy, which now became rapid. A partnership was formed, a patent granted, and the first practical telegraph was laid down for the London and Birmingham Railway, between Euston and Camden Town, within the space of a few months. This parent line consisted of five copper wires embedded in a triangular piece of wood.

Several lines were now laid down, and in 1846 the Electric Telegraph Company was incorporated. At first the venture was very unsuccessful, and the company was on the verge of ruin, when the arrest of Tawell, the Reading murderer—the first culprit "arrested by telegraph"—drew public attention to the value of the new messenger, and the electric telegraph became a commercial success.

While Cooke and Wheatstone were, in 1837, laying down their first line in England, Professor Morse was at work in America, and not only discovered a telegraph, but the admirable system of notation which bears his name, and which, with slight modification, has held its ground ever since. In other respects the original English lines have undergone considerable modification. At first, five wires and five needles were used, but it was soon discovered that by repeating the right and left movements of the needle, the alphabet could be sent equally well on two needles, or even on one.

In America, preference was given to the Morse system of registration, which consists in embossing dots and lines upon a strip of paper, and a modified form of the Morse instrument, by which the marks are made with ink, rapidly came into use in England, and now prevails throughout the world. In spite of the general success of this plan, other systems have at times obtained considerable popularity. In 1838 a patent was taken out by Mr. Edward Davy for a chemical marking telegraph. In 1846 Mr. Alexander Bain invented another system of chemical telegraphy, and also a method of perforating messages upon slips of paper, which on being drawn through a machine enable the operator to transmit intelligence at an enormous speed. Although these inventions remained in abeyance for a while, they have been recently revived by Wheatstone and others, and to the idea of using perforated slips is due the recent development of automatic telegraphy, a process by which 500 words per minute can be transmitted.

During the spread of terrestrial telegraphy, the idea that submarine cables could be laid gradually gained strength. In 1850 the first submarine cable was laid between Dover and Cape Grisnez. This consisted simply of a copper wire surrounded by gutta-percha, and enjoyed but a brief existence, owing to the interference of some fishermen, who, mistaking it for an obstinate and objectionable species of seaweed, hauled it up and cut it. In the following year a stronger cable was laid. This was made of four wires encased in gutta-percha surrounded with hemp—the whole being surrounded by spiral iron wires. The main features of this typical cable have since been closely adhered to, and the success of this and other lines produced the project of laying a cable across the Atlantic. This scheme was brought into public notice mainly by the exertions of Mr. Cyrus Field, who induced a number of London and Liverpool capitalists to subscribe £1000 apiece for the purpose of carrying it out. In 1857 the cable was laid, but, owing to the imperfect state of electrical science at that period, proved a failure. In consequence of this untoward event, a committee was appointed to inquire into the best form of submarine cable, an event in the history of science, the importance of which it is difficult to exaggerate.

Many witnesses were examined, and the outcome of the investigation was the laying of another cable in 1865. Misfortune still pursued the scheme. The second cable broke in deep water, but in 1866 a third cable was laid, and that of 1865 was cleverly picked up by Sir Samuel Canning. In the mean time a great improvement had been introduced into the construction of submarine cables by Mr. Latimer Clark (who had previously acquired celebrity by the invention of the double bell insulator). His plan consisted in encasing the cable in a covering of hemp, asphalte, and silica, applied over the iron wires so as to prevent their corrosion by the action of sea-water, an invention to which the commercial success of ocean telegraphy is in great measure to be attributed. Cables made on this plan were laid to the Isle of Man, in the Persian Gulf, and between Malta and Alexandria. Ultimately the whole Eastern world was brought into connection with England by cables stretching from Suez to Aden and Bombay, and thence to Singapore, China, and Port Darwin.

Pending the introduction of telegraphic communication between San Francisco and China, for which surveys are now being made, and which will complete the telegraphic girdle of the world, the Southern Atlantic has been crossed by a cable from Madeira to Brazil, thus bringing South America in direct communication with Lisbon, Falmouth, and London. In the work of developing the telegraphic system of the world, Englishmen have taken a prominent position. It is almost invidious to signalize a few among the many eminent engineers who have distinguished themselves in this department of their profession. Suffice it to say that in addition to those already mentioned, Sir William Thomson, Mr. Fleeming Jenkin, Mr. C. F. Varley, and Sir Charles Bright have left their mark on the history of telegraphy.

At the commencement of the present decade it was felt by many eminent electricians and members of the Institution of Civil Engineers that the department to which they had devoted themselves had at length assumed such imposing proportions as to demand a separate and special organization. Far from opposing the development of a new body, the parent society in Great George Street at once extended a helping hand to the scheme, and offered the free use of its handsome room for the meetings of the new society. To Major Frank Bolton and to Major Webber, R.E., is due the inception of the idea of a Society of Telegraph Engineers; and these gentlemen were warmly supported by Messrs. Robert Sabine, Latimer Clark, and Dr. C. W. Siemens. Between 1871 and 1872 sixty members were enrolled, among whom were Dr. C. W. Siemens, president; Lord

Lindsay and Mr. Scudamore, vice-presidents; Professor Foster, Captain Malcolm, and Captain Colomb. In the inaugural address delivered by the president, the necessity for a Society of Telegraph Engineers was eloquently insisted upon. It might have been urged against the new society that its objects were amply provided for by the institutions then in existence. In the words of the president, it might have been asked, "Is telegraph engineering not a branch of civil engineering, and do not all our proceedings, therefore, fall within the legitimate sphere of action of the Institution of Civil Engineers? Or, if we meet with difficult questions in physical or mathematical science, is not the Royal Society or Section A of the British Association open for us to discuss them, or may we not go before the Institution of Mechanical Engineers with any purely mechanical question? Is it desirable, indeed, it may be urged, to take a branch from the parent stem and to cultivate it separately? Shall we not degenerate thereby into 'specialists,' or what may be called 'fractional quantities of scientific men,' and this in the face of the patent fact that the further we advance in scientific knowledge (whether pure or applied) the more clearly we perceive the intimate connection between its different branches, and the impossibility of cultivating one without constantly reverting to the others?"

These possible objections were disposed of in the following admirable apology for specialism:—"If it is impossible for one man to master the special knowledge accumulated in different branches of engineering science, it would be equally impossible for one society to cultivate all those branches in detail; thus the Royal Society can only entertain questions involving general principles of science, and is obliged to leave questions of exhaustive research to special societies; questions of minute chemical investigation are assigned to the Chemical Society; questions regarding the orbits of celestial bodies to the Astronomical Society; and by the same rule of limitation the Royal Society would refuse to receive, for instance, a paper on testing the joints of insulated wire, which would be a subject peculiarly suited for our Society. The Institution of Civil Engineers has, on the other hand, received, at certain intervals of time (varying from two to three years), a general paper on the progress of telegraph engineering; but it is self-evident that such an occasional paper must be quite inadequate to constitute a record of the progress of a branch of engineering which gives daily proof of its public importance, which is distinguished for its rapid development, and which comprises within itself a wide range of scientific inquiry; nor would there be time, on such rare occasions, to discuss questions of detail which are of special interest to the telegraph engineer."

It was at once felt that it was most desirable to secure the support of men occupying influential positions in the great telegraphic systems of the world. As the world was already bound together by a great network of international telegraphy traversing deserts and mountain chains, the deep plateau of the Atlantic, and the more dangerous bottoms of tropical seas, it was very properly deemed necessary that the Society of Telegraph Engineers should be made a cosmopolitan institution—a focus into which the thoughts and observations of all countries might flow, in order to be again radiated in every direction, for the general advancement of science. To carry out this view, the practice of admitting foreign members—which has shed no little glory on many cognate societies—was adopted. Among the first to respond to the invitations of the Society were General von Lüders, Director-General of the Imperial Russian Telegraphs; Signor D'Amico, Director-General of Telegraphs in Italy; M. Ailhaud, Inspector-General of Telegraphic Lines in France; M. Vinchant, Inspector-General of Public Works in Belgium; M. Hippolyte Aranjo, of Spain; and Professor Campanena, the Director-General of Brazilian Telegraphs.

In pursuance of this wise policy—imitating that of

the Institution of Civil Engineers—the new Society now proceeded to enrol honorary members, notably Sir George Airy, K.C.B., Astronomer Royal, General Sir Edward Sabine, and Professor Weber. The publication of a journal embodying the proceedings of the Society was the next object of solicitude. It was at first hoped that this important record of telegraphy might be published in the three most important languages of Europe; but this idea—admirable in itself—was subsequently abandoned, and the *Journal* now appears, like those of other learned societies, simply in English. The Society went to work with a will. So early as the session of 1872 was read a paper on "Automatic Telegraphy"—a subject now engaging the earnest attention of the telegraphic world —by Mr. R. S. Culley. During the same session an interesting discussion on "Sea Telegraphy" was induced by an able paper read by Captain Colomb, R.N. Army telegraphs were also discoursed upon by Captain Malcolm, and the application of Colmar's calculating machine to electrical computation was explained by Mr. C. Bruce Warren.

During the session 1872-73 many papers of great interest were read, among which may be cited the following:—"On Military Telegraphs in connection with the Autumn Manœuvres," "On Lightning and Lightning Conductors," "On the Application of Iron to Telegraph Poles," and on "Earth Currents." The "Block System" also came in for a large share of attention, the reading and discussion of papers on this important subject having occupied several meetings of the Society.

The proceedings of the Society are recorded in the *Journal of the Society of Telegraph Engineers*, which contains, moreover, much valuable matter in the form of abstracts, translations, and original communications, and is admirably edited by the hon. sec., Major Frank Bolton, and the secretary, Mr. G. E. Preece. Among other valuable matter contained in its pages will be found copies of the photographic records of the various magnetic disturbances in the great magnetic storm of February 4th, 1872, contributed by the Astronomer Royal, and a "Register of the Computed Force and the Direction of Earth Currents observed at Valentia during 78 Days—from March 6th to May 22nd, 1871, upon 1850 nauts of cable." This table is not only curious and valuable in itself, but is remarkable as an instance of ingenious editing. Mr. Preece considering that in printing a table containing 3744 numerical statements—encumbered moreover by stars, dots, and dashes—the chances of error were very great, cut the knot by having the original document photographed and the prints inserted in the *Journal*.

The Society of Telegraph Engineers has grown as

rapidly as the science it represents. The original sixty members have now increased to 580. These consist of Members, Associates, Students, Foreign Members, and Honorary Members, governed by a Council composed of the president—Sir Wm. Thomson—the two past presidents—Mr. Scudamore and Dr. C. W. Siemens—four vice-presidents, twelve other members, and three Associates. In the case of any person desiring to become a full Member, certain qualifications are very properly insisted on. He must have been regularly educated as a telegraph engineer, and have had subsequent employment for at least five years in responsible situations; or have practised on his own account as a telegraph engineer for at least two years, and have acquired a certain degree of eminence in the profession; or be so intimately associated with the science of electricity or the progress of telegraphy that the Council consider his admission to membership would conduce to the interests of the Society.

Less rigid conditions are exacted in the case of Associates, who need only to be persons of more than twenty-one years of age whose pursuits constitute branches of electrical engineering, or who are intimately associated with the science of electricity or the progress of telegraphy.

Studentship is accorded to pupils under eighteen and not over twenty-one years of age. Foreign and

Honorary Members are admitted on the conditions common to other scientific institutions.

Applicants for admission to the Society having been proposed and seconded in writing, and the application having been first submitted by the secretary to the Council, are elected by ballot—two-thirds of the members voting being required to secure election. Honorary Members only are elected by the Council without appeal to the general body. Every Member contributes two guineas, every Associate one guinea, every Foreign Member one pound, and every Student half-a-guinea annually to the Society. The session commences in November and ends in June, and the meetings still take place—thanks to the courtesy of the parent institution—in the great room of the Institution of Civil Engineers, Great George Street, Westminster. These meetings resemble so closely those of the Civil Engineers, that it is needless for me to dwell upon the details of procedure. The discussions are always lively and suggestive—as might be expected at a meeting of the professors of a youthful science, marvellous enough in its already revealed power, but doubly interesting from its magnificent possibilities.

XI.

THE MUSEUM OF PRACTICAL GEOLOGY.

Extending from Jermyn Street to Piccadilly is a handsome and commodious building which affords, perhaps, the best example in this country of what a museum ought to be. To begin with, it was built for a special purpose, and is not a conversion or adaptation of a structure originally intended for something else. Although containing objects which, from their industrial importance alone, are interesting to all sorts and conditions of men, the Museum of Practical Geology is really and truly a museum in the highest and best acceptation of the word. It is not a mere collection of geological specimens prettily arranged to catch the eye and tickle the fancy of fashionable dabblers in the 'ologies, but is a superbly organized exhibition of the minerals of the British Islands, arranged with direct reference to their employment in manufactures and to the instruction of students in their geographical distribution, geological formation, chemical and mineralogical character, and metallurgical treatment. This educational element is strengthened by metallurgical laboratories, and by the combination of the Royal School of Mines, to a certain extent, with the Museum. Mr. Pennethorne's handsome structure might, indeed, be described in the manner of Mrs. Malaprop as "three institutions at once." The Royal School of Mines has been dealt with in a previous paper, and the Mining Record Office, a most valuable institution, may be described in a few words. The objects to which it is devoted are the collection, arrangement, and preservation of all sections of mines and collieries now in work or abandoned, the collection of every kind of information connected with the mineral formations of the United Kingdom, and the collection and publication of mining statistics. It is unnecessary for me to descant upon the importance of these functions, or on the admirable manner in which they are performed, as the public is perfectly familiar with the Annual Statistical Return of the mineral produce of the British Islands, prepared by Mr. Robert Hunt, F.R.S., Keeper of Mining Records, and author, in conjunction with Mr. F. W. Rudler, of an admirable descriptive Guide to the Museum of Practical Geology.

The triple institution in Jermyn Street is the direct outgrowth of the Geological Survey of the United Kingdom, commenced at first on his own account by Sir Henry Thomas de la Beche, and afterwards adopted by the Government. Having induced the Government to undertake this important work, Sir H. de la Beche lost no time in suggesting that the survey itself would supply means for collecting specimens of the applications of geology to the useful purposes of life. The importance of a museum which should illustrate the mineral productions of the country and show their commercial value was immediately recognized, and apartments at No. 6, Craig's Court, appointed to receive the nucleus of the present splendid collection. At first called the "Museum of Economic Geology," the collection soon became important enough to need the services of a curator, and in 1839 Mr. Richard Phillips, F.R.S., was appointed to that office. Being an able chemist, Mr. Phillips was induced to unite analytical investigations with his duties as curator. No sooner was a laboratory established and regular work commenced, than students sought admittance. At first only a limited number could be favoured, but the ultimate result of this wise addition of scientific demonstration to a special museum was the establishment of the Royal School of Mines.

The museum in Jermyn Street was opened on May 14th, 1851, by His Royal Highness the late Prince Consort, and in its construction was made to illustrate some of the objects in view. The Piccadilly front is of Anston (Yorkshire) dolomite, or magnesian limestone, and the Jermyn Street front is composed partly of the same stone and partly of Suffolk bricks; the steps at the entrance are of red Peterhead granite, at the doorway is a slab of Penrhyn slate, the pavement and steps leading into the hall are of Portland stone, the base of the sides of the vestibules is of Irish granite, the upper portion of polished Derbyshire alabaster, and the pilasters of grey Peterhead granite.

The specimens are admirably arranged in separate lines of cases placed in such juxtaposition that the progress of any one metalliferous mineral may be traced from the geological stratum whence the ore is extracted through the various processes of manufacture till the metal ultimately assumes the forms required for use or ornament. Thus, the natural materials may be studied as to their lithological character, their geological order, or their mineralogical constitution; the artificial productions, exhibiting the results of labour and science, may be investigated in a commercial, scientific, or artistic spirit; the models of mechanical appliances reveal the means by which industrial results are attained; while a valuable collection of foreign and colonial minerals affords opportunities of comparing these with native produce, and a selection of historical specimens illustrates the progress of metallurgy and the art of working in metals in all countries and in all ages.

To that most important of all metals—iron—much space is naturally devoted. Among the many specimens of British iron ores, the valuable red hæmatite is represented by samples from Ulverstone and Whitehaven, where the development of the iron industry has, within a short space, enriched and populated a region previously remarkable for picturesqueness and poverty. The crystallized variety called specular ore, or iron-glance, is illustrated by specimens from Cleator Moor, where it occurs in cavities in the compact ore, and the micaceous iron ores of Devon and Anglesey are also well illustrated.

The abundant and widely-diffused limonite or brown iron ore is also represented. From the earliest times this well-known mineral has been raised in the Forest of Dean, which, however, is only one of the many localities in which it is found in this country. From Cornwall come magnificent specimens of a variety of brown ore, called göthite—a crystallized hydrous peroxide of iron. Many fine samples appear of the brown iron ores of the secondary strata, especially those of the lias and the overlaying oolites.

These ores have, within the last quarter of a century, acquired immense importance. Among the most celebrated is the Cleveland ironstone, the main body of which is a carbonate of the protoxide of iron, the upper part of the deposit passing into brown ore. This famous stratum—upon which the industry of a now wealthy and thickly-populated district depends—was discovered in 1848-49 on the north-eastern coast of Yorkshire. "From Redcar to Middlesborough-on-Tees, there crops out a solid stratum no less than fifteen feet thick. This remarkable ironstone seam extends over a region of some hundreds of square miles. It is capped by sandy shales containing scattered nodules of ironstone, and ultimately—above the marlstone series to which it belongs—by the upper lias shale, so well known along the Whitby coast for its fossils, jet, and the application of some of the beds to the manufacture of alum." The Northamptonshire and Lincolnshire ironstones are also extensively worked. The first-named occurs in the Northampton Sand, at the base of the Great Oolite, while the Lincolnshire ironstone—like that of Cleveland—is found in the Marlstone or Middle Lias.

In carbonates of iron England is less rich than many foreign countries, but fine specimens of spathose ore come from the Brendon Hills, in Somersetshire, and from Weardale, in Durham. When associated with certain argillaceous impurities impeding its crystallization, this carbonate of iron becomes the well-known clay ironstone, which, although hardly entitled to rank as a distinct mineralogical species—and therefore destitute of purely scientific interest—is of great commercial value from its distribution through South Wales, North Wales, Shropshire, South Staffordshire, Warwickshire, North Staffordshire, Yorkshire, Derbyshire, and the northern counties. Among these clay ironstones are samples of the famous carbonaceous ironstone known as "black band," from which the largest quantity of Scotch iron is made. This ore, which was discovered in 1801 by Mr. Mushet, is frequently called "Mushet stone."

Among the foreign and colonial iron ores are the Canadian bog ore, the richer magnetic ore, and titaniferous iron, which occur in large quantities in the Dominion. Of great interest also are numerous specimens of the magnetic iron ores of Sweden. These are distributed over an area of 16,000 square miles. The best iron is obtained from the Dannemora mines, and large quantities are exported to England, where they are employed at Sheffield and other places for making steel. Beautiful specimens of specular iron ore are contributed by the Isle of Elba, where enormous deposits occur. This ore, famous even in remote antiquity, has long been worked by large open excavations. Elba also possesses rich veins of magnetic ore, associated with hæmatite, at the famous Loadstone Mountain, or Monte Calamita. Specimens of brown iron ore come from many countries, but more interesting than these are the blocks of spathose from Dauphiné, Styria, Carinthia, and last, but not least, from the neighbourhood of Siegen, in Rhenish Prussia, including the celebrated Stahlberg, near Müsen. During the last few years the importance of these spathic ores has enormously increased, owing to the growing demand for spiegeleisen—indispensable to the manufacture of Bessemer steel.

Proceeding from the geology, chemistry, distribution, and value of the raw material, to the varied processes employed in reducing iron from the ore, the visitor finds this part of the subject profusely illustrated. The metallurgical specimens in the East Indian cases are full of interest. "Wootz," or Indian steel, is manufactured by the natives chiefly from magnetic ores. The smelting apparatus is very rude —consisting of a small open furnace, in which the ore is disposed in layers of small pieces alternating with layers of charcoal. The blast is provided by two small bellows made of goat-skins, and the metal when reduced falls into a hole at the bottom of the furnace and forms a cake of malleable iron. "To convert this into 'wootz,' a small wedge is cut from the iron cake and placed with pieces of dry wood in a clay crucible, which is heated in a rude furnace until the iron becomes carbonized." On breaking open the crucible the steel is found at the bottom in the form of the small conical cakes exhibited in case 38. The quantity of iron produced in this primitive way would provoke a smile from the lords of many blast-furnaces. In Oldham's Report on the Damoodah Valley, 1852, when East Indian iron-making was more actively pursued than at the present time, it is stated that the whole district employed 70 furnaces, producing nearly 2380 tons of pig-iron per annum!

After the model-room, containing models of blast-furnaces and blowing engines, has been inspected, the numerous specimens of English pig-iron demand attention. Here are samples of hot and of cold blast pig—grey, mottled, and white—from the Whitehaven Works in Cumberland, from the Lowmoor, Bowling, and Farnley Works in Yorkshire, from the Russell's Hall Works in South Staffordshire, from the Plymouth, Dowlais, and Maesteg Works in Glamorganshire, and from Monklands, Lanarkshire.

The interesting process of steel-making may be studied to great advantage at the Museum of Practical Geology. At the north end of the museum is a model of a Sheffield steel manufactory, including furnaces, rolling mills, and forge; and not far from this is one of the most beautifully executed models in existence. It represents the whole apparatus employed in making Bessemer steel, and, previous to its presentation to the Museum by Mr. Bessemer, was exhibited at the International Exhibition at Paris, in 1867, where it gained a prize. This model alone would repay a visit to Jermyn Street. Numerous specimens of mild steel are exhibited, and one stand contains specimens of every variety of steel sent into the market. Every stage of manufacture is illustrated. There is the puddled and rolled iron bar—recarbonized by "cementation"—and then known as "blister steel," while near at hand are specimens of blister steel, which, by various welding processes, have been advanced to the condition of "half shear," "single shear," "double shear," and "faggot steel." Fine blocks of cast steel revive the agreeable thought that the very difficult trade of making cast steel has at last revived. The manufacture of sheet and bar steel is not overlooked, nor are specimens wanting to indicate the various processes of hardening and tempering. In case 41 is found an interesting series of specimens of steel at the different colours for tempering. Beautiful samples of steel springs are shown. One of these—a miniature spring for a tiny watch—weighs but 0·125 of a grain—and being commercially worth about 25s., was used by Babbage as an illustration of the value of labour. Here is indeed an instance of an inappreciable and almost invisible quantity of material acquiring a high value simply from the time and labour spent in its production.

Whitworth's screws and plates are also wonderful examples of technical skill. The celebrated plates are of considerable weight, but when the two iron planes are brought together, and the air between them expelled by simple pressure, the cohesive force of the two surfaces is so great that the plates may be lifted from the ground by the handle of the upper one—a conclusive proof of the correctness with which the surfaces have been formed. Near these triumphs of accurate workmanship are some fine examples of Berlin iron castings. Many beautiful specimens also come from the ironworks of Count de Stolberg-Wernigerode, at Ilsenburg, Hartz Mountains. One large ornamental casting is exhibited with the sand attached as it was taken from the mould.

In table-case 48 is a fine collection of ancient and modern Oriental and Western sword-blades. Swords and daggers from the Punjaub, Ispahan, and Borneo repose peacefully side by side with the blades of Damascus and Toledo, and the masterpieces of sword-making said to have been tempered by Andrea Ferrara in the remote solitude of a Highland glen. From the earliest periods Oriental sword-blades have been justly celebrated. Among these the Damascus blades held the first rank and were remarkable for their keenness of edge, great flexibility, a peculiar waviness or fleckiness always observed on the surface, and a musky odour said to be given out on the blade being bent or rubbed.

Without attempting to cut the knotty arguments with which the Damascus question is involved, I may simply say that the excellence of Eastern blades is easily accounted for. In the East people are not in a hurry. Over their wonderful textile fabrics and on their hammered metal, they are content to forget that there is such a thing as time. Even unto this day the excellent iron ores of Asia are reduced by charcoal, and, although I know this remark to be absurd from a commercial point of view, I am not afraid to say that things made singly and by hand—without regard to time—are very likely to be better in quality than those turned out by the thousand. The system does not "pay," I suppose; but I have my doubts whether work of the best kind, honestly, conscientiously, and thoroughly performed, does often actually "pay" in immediate hard cash. I have seen two or three specimens of metal-work, produced in these latter days, which have occupied ten years of a man's life to complete. The *artifex* was paid an immense price, but let us think of the time occupied in earning the money! The result is work unequalled, unapproachable, but whether it literally, and in a vulgar sense, "paid" the patient toiler for the time and genius expended is very doubtful.

In case 13 is shown the modern process of sword manufacture as practised at Birmingham. From Sheffield comes a large quantity of bars of steel called "sword-moulds." To the mould is fastened the tang, which is of iron. The result of the different stages of forging is very clearly shown, and also the effect of tempering the blade by drawing it through the fire several times until the surface exhibits a bluish oxidation. Another very interesting case is that illustrating the development of a first-class gun-barrel from a heap of horse-shoe nails. Great care is devoted to the arrangement of this case, and the advance of nails to bars, the twisting of these on a mandril, and the subsequent welding and boring operations are beautifully illustrated.

Less important metals than iron have received equally conscientious treatment at the hands of Mr. Hunt, Mr. Trenham Reeks, and Mr. Rudler, who are deservedly proud of the masterly arrangement of the Museum. Copper may be traced from the yellow, purple, and grey copper ores through all the complex processes of smelting to the evolution of bar copper, and the conversion of this into sheets. The malleability of copper is also well shown in a fine series of examples of the gradual development of a copper vase of elegant form from a disc of metal. A magnificent mass of native copper is also to be seen. The frequent occurrence of virgin malleable copper has been advanced by many writers on metals as a reason why copper was employed for many ages before iron.

Unfortunately for this theory it has recently been shown that iron was in use in Egypt at the time of the Pharoahs, and in India from time immemorial; while an Assyrian tripod ring in the Museum of Practical Geology (case 20) demonstrates, to the satisfaction of Dr. Percy, that the bronze had been cast round a support of iron, by which means the appearance of lightness was attained, and great strength was ensured. Advocates of the new theory assert, with great plausibility, that the rapid oxidation of iron explains its absence from very ancient monuments.

In like manner the processes employed in the reduction of other metals are profusely illustrated in a series of cases. Superb specimens of the raw material are shown, among which I may cite a very instructive piece of a lead vein from the Grassington mines in Yorkshire, and a portion of a vein of gold-bearing quartz from Grass Valley, Nevada County, California.

A large horse-shoe case in the first gallery contains a classified collection of the minerals once designated non-metalliferous. Chief among these rank the diamond and the "black diamond." A superb snuff-box, presented to the late Sir Roderick Murchison by the Emperor Nicholas of Russia, and bequeathed by the recipient to the Museum, occupies a place of honour among many other specimens of pure carbon. Less beautiful, but far more important than the diamond, is the great modern motive power—coal. The varieties of coal form a regular series, commencing with hard coal, or anthracite, and passing through the ordinary bituminous coals to the more recently-formed lignite. Here are numerous specimens of true anthracite, of cannel coal, lignite, and jet, of the curious mineral known as Bog-Head cannel, and of Kimmeridge coal and other hydro-carbons, such as asphalt, elaterite, and amber. Considerable space is devoted to coal and to the method of "winning" it. There are models of the "surface workings of a Newcastle coalpit," of the "Shipley Colliery in Derbyshire," and of the different modes of working and ventilating coal mines. In addition to these are found one of Ridley and Co's coal-cutting machines, and specimens of the tools employed in various mining districts. Immediately above the coal-cutting machine is an interesting collection of ancient Saxon mining axes, richly ornamented. These formed the badges of office among the chief miners, and were only carried on State occasions. It is curious to trace the gradual steps by which a miner's axe became by degrees more highly ornamented and reduced in weight, until at length the ancient axe shrank to the dimensions of a practicable walking stick—a mere wand of office.

In case 5, in the model room, is a complete collection of mining lamps, showing the inventions of Davy and Stephenson, and the improvements subsequently made in them, among which is the remarkable magnet-lamp invented to prevent the miner from opening his lamp to light his pipe.

In the upper gallery is a fine collection of British fossils, admirably arranged for the use of students; but it is impossible to do more than allude to the numerous objects of interest in the Museum of Practical Geology. Several cases in the hall are filled with polished cubes of British ornamental stones, collected to assist the deliberations of the Building-Stone Commissioners appointed to select the best possible stone for building the present Houses of Parliament. An immense deal of trouble was taken in testing the physical and chemical properties of the various stones, but the selection arrived at can hardly be designated a success. Another most interesting relic is a portion of the boulder-stone used for the sarcophagus of the late Duke of Wellington. A huge boulder had long lain supine in a field in Cornwall, to the despair of the farmer, who on several occasions proposed to blow it up, but was deterred by the menaces of the country folk, who, by addressing him thus—"If thee shoots that, we'll shoot thee," succeeded in preserving the stone to fulfil its great destiny. A series of handsome busts adorns the hall of the Museum. Appropriately carved in stone are the counterfeit presentments of great geologists. An important addition to the busts of Smith, Playfair, De la Beche, Buckland, and Murchison, has recently been presented to the Museum by a generous lady. This is a magnificent marble bust of the late Professor Sedgwick, by Woolner—one of the happiest efforts of that eminent sculptor. Out of the main track of the visitor is a curious and valuable collection, illustrative of the progress of fictile industry in this country and abroad. The ceramic and vitreous series contains specimens of Bovey clay, Poole clay, China stone, and the famous Kaolin, China or Cornish clay, to the introduction of which the beauty of porcelain is mainly to be attributed. Specimens of raw material and of various kinds of porcelain and pottery, in different stages of manufacture, are arranged on the symmetrical plan carried out in every other department; but, albeit proud of their handsome collection of china and glass, the courteous officers of the institution confess with sorrow that perhaps their well-meant efforts have contributed to excite the present absurd mania for crockery.

The Museum is open gratuitously to the public on Mondays and Saturdays from 10 a.m. to 10 p.m., and on the other days of the week (Friday excepted) during the usual hours. There is one month of vacation, from the 10th August to the 10th September, when the Museum is entirely closed.

The edifice contains a library of 15,000 volumes, devoted to the sciences taught in the School of Mines. These are available for the use of students in the School, and also, upon special application, stating the object in view, may be consulted by other inquirers.

Taken altogether, the institution in Jermyn Street is admirable. As a "show" it is full of interest and entertainment, but considered in its more important aspect as an engine of direct instruction, it not only excites admiration at its perfect arrangement, but wonder that no greater haste is made to follow the excellent example set by the Museum of Practical Geology.

XII.

THE BRITISH ASSOCIATION FOR THE ADVANCEMENT OF SCIENCE.

FORASMUCH as the British Association is only conspicuous in London by its absence, and holds its meetings everywhere but in the metropolis, it can hardly be included under the title of "Scientific London." Still, when I reflect that much of the work of this important body is done on the banks of the Thames, and that committee meetings take place in Albemarle Street, while the great holiday gatherings are reserved for the provinces, I cannot refrain from mentioning a society of special type, which has exercised enormous influence in disseminating and fostering a natural taste for every branch of science.

With the advent of the spirit of scientific investigation arose the idea that while the formation of special societies would assist the development of particular branches of study, some great catholic association should promote the general advance of science in this country. For a long while this duty was fulfilled by the Royal Society. From the collection of detached facts and observations this august body advanced at length to the pursuit of knowledge of all kinds, and accepting communications on every branch of science, filled the important position of supreme arbiter of the scientific circles of England.

But in time the limbs grew too numerous and too ponderous for the parent trunk, and were lopped off one by one. The Society of Antiquaries disposed of one class of communications, and the Linnæan Society, the Geological and Royal Astronomical Societies successively reduced the area of the Royal Society's work. Meanwhile scientific knowledge advanced and entirely new sciences sprang into existence.

At the commencement of the present century the brilliant discoveries and attractive lectures of Davy had forced from society a species of recognition, while the extraordinary development of the steam-engine, and the increasing trade in dyes and other "chemicals," had brought home to the commercial mind the importance of scientific knowledge. It became recognized that the very existence of England depends on her being second to no other nation in the prompt application of scientific discoveries and scientific method to the gigantic industries for which this little island is celebrated. For a while the antagonistic influence of two widely separated sections of society was severely felt. On the part of the great Universities a positive dislike was shown to the introduction of science into education. At the University of Oxford, the elegant—but utterly useless—trick of composing Greek and Latin verse was considered of sufficient importance to occupy several of the most valuable years of a man's life; while at Cambridge—invested with scientific glory by the immortal Newton—although mathematical science enjoyed a certain prominence, its study was almost exclusively regarded as a mere training of the understanding, a species of mental gymnastics fitted to harden the logical faculties as practice in the eight-oar hardens and develops the muscles. As an instrument for the discovery of new truths, mathematics were entirely disregarded, and Cambridge was content to let science be where it was left by the great philosopher who described himself as a child picking up shells by the shore of the ocean of truth. Those impressed with the value of a scientific education, groaned over the Oxford graduate, whose proficiency in the dead languages was compensated by complete ignorance of the elementary principles of a telescope, a barometer, or a steam-engine, and declared that unless scientific study were made compulsory as an integral part of an university education, neither Oxford nor Cambridge would ever become the scene of scientific investigation.

We all now know how science has triumphed over her foes in the Universities, but it is deeply interesting to consider how much progress has been retarded on the other hand by the so-called "practical man." Whether a general officer or a blacksmith, the "practical man" sternly opposed any application of theoretical knowledge to his peculiar profession. The natural bull-headedness of Englishmen made the English practical man peculiarly offensive. It was often asked, "Of what use is science?" and the head of a great military department once declared openly that he "hated scientific officers," while it was but too well known that in his own department more money had been wasted and more lives lost—from sheer ignorance of science—"than any one could think of without shame and sorrow." Another general officer—as if to justify Fielding's remarks on the military cranium—gave it as his opinion that "theoretical knowledge was not necessary in the army. An officer might be a good officer without any education at all."

In the industrial world a like feeling prevailed. Dr. Lyon Playfair declared that the title of "practical man" was erroneously used by Englishmen to envelop their ignorance, and that reliance on the "practical or common sense of our population is the sunken rock directly in the course both of our agriculture and manufactures." Dr. Lyon Playfair continued in the following terms:—"If England keeps pace with other countries as a manufacturing nation, it must be by her sons of industry becoming humble disciples of science. Now that the progress of human events has converted the competition of industry into a competition of intellect, it will no longer do to plume and pride ourselves on our power of mere practical adaptation. It is miserable to see our industrial population glorying in their ignorance of the principles on which their manufactures depend, and vaunting their empiricism, or, as they term it, their practice."

The importance of applying the faculties of observation and reasoning to the problems of nature is also proclaimed by Sir John Herschel, who says, "The abstract sciences are the concentration of what has been established as true in the operations of nature—they are so much of certainty acquired in the midst of uncertainty. When sufficiently advanced to be directly applicable to the industrial and other arts they convert the crawl of improvement into a race." Theory may, then, be defined as a species of rule of which practice is merely the example; but, for all that, is yet at a discount in this country, where people love to ignore their obligations to such "theorists" as

Newton, Watt, Stephen Gray, and Davy, and to exalt to the skies the "practical men" who blundered and muddled on for thousands of years without achieving any great improvement, and would probably have gone on stumbling for ever had not the gloomy regions of practice been illumined by the light of theory.

The influence of the numerous learned societies in encouraging observation and diffusing a philosophical spirit, the efforts of the Royal Society to excite interest in purely scientific subjects, and the excellent work done by the Society of Arts in showing the intimate connection between science and industry, failed to secure national appreciation until steam communication and the rapid transmission of news by degrees made men aware of the enormous losses of life and property annually suffered from sheer want of scientific knowledge. Pending the more general appreciation of the advantages of scientific culture, a discussion arose, between the years 1826 and 1831, on the low state of science and scientific men in England.

To Sir David Brewster is undoubtedly due the origin of the British Association, but the original conception of a Scientific Parliament is purely German, and was simply imported into this country by the great northern philosopher. In 1822 Dr. Oken, of Munich, originated the idea of an annual congress of scientific men, with the object of bringing them into personal contact. The first meeting was held at Leipzig, and was attended by only thirty-two persons, of whom twenty were resident in the city. The meetings, however, rapidly increased in importance. That of 1827, held in Munich, was warmly patronised by the King of Bavaria, and in the following year the philosophers assembled at Berlin, on which occasion they were warmly welcomed by the King and presided over by the illustrious Von Humboldt. Babbage was the only Englishman present, and communicated an interesting account of the Scientific Congress to the *Edinburgh Journal of Science*.

Intelligent foreigners had long remarked the slender estimation in which science and its votaries were held in England, and by the efforts of Sir Humphry Davy, Sir John Herschel, Sir David Brewster, and others, the upper stratum of national feeling was stirred up. It was set forth that foreign scientific institutions were greatly superior to those in existence in England, and the decline of scientific studies among the aristocracy was vigorously pointed out by Davy, who remarked that, "in looking back to the history of the last five reigns in England, we find Boyles, Cavendishes, and Howards, who rendered their great names more illustrious by their scientific renown, but we may in vain search the aristocracy now for philosophers; and there are very few persons who pursue science with true dignity; it is followed more as connected with objects of profit than those of fame, and there are fifty persons who take out patents for supposed inventions for one who makes a real discovery." In like spirit, Babbage exposed the prevailing ignorance of the more difficult and abstract sciences, and declared that mathematics and, with it, the highest departments of physical science had gradually declined since the days of Newton. These shortcomings were attributed to the abuses then existing in the management of our scientific institutions—the imperfect system of instruction in public schools and universities—the ignorance of public men—and the culpable indifference of successive Governments to the intellectual glory of the country. Babbage's onslaught was supported by Sir David Brewster, who, in the *Quarterly Review*, drew a comparison between the existing state of science at home and abroad, very much to the disadvantage of England. At the conclusion of this important article, the writer—whose philosophic investigations had extended through every branch of physical science—mentioned the best method for reviving and extending science in the British Islands:—"An Association of our nobility, clergy, gentry, and philosophers can alone draw the attention of the Sovereign and the nation to this blot upon its fame." In 1831, through the instrumentality of Lord

Brougham, the state of science and its followers was brought before Lord Grey's Government, and some important objects relative to the Association suggested by Sir David Brewster were secured.

Early in 1831 Sir David Brewster set vigorously to work to establish a *British Association of Men of Science,* similar to that which had existed for eight years in Germany. The principal objects of the Society were to make the cultivators of science familiar with each other, to stimulate one another to new exertions, to bring the objects of science before the public eye, and to take measures for advancing its interests and accelerating its progress. York was selected by Sir David Brewster as the locality for the first meeting, on the ground of its being a central town already provided with a Philosophical Society of its own. The local philosophers as well as the mayor and magistrates of York took up the project heartily, and the first meeting was attended by more than three hundred persons, who responded to the invitations issued by the Yorkshire Philosophical Society. Prominent among the organizers of the movement were Sir Roderick Murchison, Professor Phillips, and Rev. W. Vernon Harcourt in London, and Messrs. Robinson, Johnston, and Forbes in Edinburgh, while the learned and venerable Archbishop of York entered warmly and hospitably into the scheme. Under the presidency of Lord Milton the inaugural meeting was held at the Museum of the York Philosophical Society, the British Association was duly organized; and so well was the important task of planning and arranging performed that few variations have been made from the original sketch.

Thoroughly maintaining the idea of catholicity, the British Association contemplates no interference with the ground occupied by other institutions. Briefly stated its objects are:—To give a stronger impulse and a more systematic direction to scientific inquiry—to promote the intercourse of those who cultivate science in different parts of the British Empire with one another and with foreign philosophers—to obtain a more general attention to the objects of science, and a removal of any disadvantages of a public kind which impede its progess. The Association meets annually for at least one week in some town decided upon two years in advance. During the forty-three years of its existence the members of the Association have indeed seen men and cities. Not only the great commercial centres of the kingdom, but seats of learning and fashionable watering-places have been visited. Thus Oxford, Dublin, Liverpool, York, Cambridge, Bath, Glasgow and Cheltenham, Brighton and Bradford, have in turn welcomed the British Association. On the occasion of these visits ample preparations are made by the local authorities, and much hospitality dispensed. At Bradford last year, for instance, the city expended some £3,000 in receiving and entertaining the philosophers.

After the general meeting, at which the president-elect delivers an address, the general committee takes the business of the meeting in hand, while particular departments are discussed in the sections by special committees. The sections into which the business of the British Association is divided are—A. Mathematical and Physical Science. B. Chemical Science. C. Geology. D. Biology—subdivided into three departments—Anatomy and Physiology—Zoology and Botany—Anthropology. E. Geography. F. Economic Science and Statistics. G. Mechanical Science.

In these sections the proceedings of the previous annual meeting, the recommendations adopted there, and the action since taken upon them, are reviewed. Suggestions are also made by the members, and definite points of research to which individual or combined exertion may be usefully directed, are carefully selected after due discussion. Many interesting papers are read, and of these the most interesting are published *in extenso* in the annual report, while those of less importance receive the slighter honour of an extract.

During the annual celebration two evenings are

to be one of the most arbitrary and irregular of all crimes. In point of fact, it is nothing of the kind. Murder is commited with as much regularity, and bears as uniform a relation to certain known circumstances as do the movements of the tides and the rotations of the seasons. In the words of the greatest statist whom the world has yet seen, "in everything which concerns crime, the same numbers re-occur with a constancy which it would be impossible to misunderstand, even in the case of those crimes which seem quite independent of human foresight, such for instance as murders, which are generally committed after quarrels arising from circumstances apparently fortuitous. Nevertheless, experience proves that not only the same number of murders takes place every year, but that even the instruments by which they are committed are employed in the same proportion." This language was used in 1835 by the illustrious thinker who spent his useful life in collecting and methodizing the statistics of different countries. Later inquiries have confirmed these generalizations so completely as to have induced the observation that "the uniform reproduction of crime is more clearly marked and more capable of being predicted than are the physical laws connected with the disease and destruction of our bodies." Suicide, apparently the most eccentric of crimes, and that which depends more than any other upon individual will, and less upon surrounding circumstances, has been shown to be merely the product of the general condition of society: "All appears to depend upon predetermined causes. Thus we find yearly almost the same number of suicides, not only in general, but in distinguishing sex, age, and methods of self-destruction. One year reproduces so faithfully the figures of the year which preceded it that it is possible to predict what will happen the year after." But it is not only the graver crimes of mankind that are marked by a terrible uniformity of sequence. Minor indiscretions follow the same iron law. Marriage was once supposed to be determined by the temper and caprice of individuals, but the statist has shown that the number of marriages annually contracted is determined not by Jack and Jill but by large general facts over which obscure units exercise slight authority.

Marriages are now known to bear a fixed and definite relation to the price of corn, and "the experience of a century has proved that, instead of having any connection with personal feelings, they are simply regulated by the average earnings of the great mass of the people; so that this immense social and religious institution is not only swayed but completely controlled by the price of food and the rate of wages." Another curious instance is the necessary and invariable order of aberration of memory. Twenty years ago the post-offices of London and Paris published returns of the number of letters which the writers, through forgetfulness, had omitted to direct, and the result has been a proof that, year after year, the same proportion of letter-writers forget this simple act; so that, for each successive period, we can actually foretell the number of persons whose memory will fail them in directing a letter, with a near approach to the accuracy with which we can predict the occurrence of an eclipse or the advent of a comet.

To statists, then, belongs the merit of first disclosing the action of great general laws upon the moral as well as on the physical world, by bringing to bear upon it that powerful engine for eliciting truth—the science of numbers. Mainly employed in investigating the condition of man himself, the statist leaves the distribution of land and water to the geographer, the constitution of the earth's crust to the geologist, the description of man, as an individual organism, to the physiologist, his position in contrast to that of other animals to the anthropologist, his relation to other races of men to the ethnologist, and concerns himself with man, viewed as a citizen and a proprietor. The principle lying at the foundation of statistics is, then, that the laws which govern nature, and more especially those which determine the moral and physical condition of mankind, are constant, and are to be discovered by the accurate and patient investigation and comparison of phenomena extending over a large number of instances. Accidental diversities diminish in importance as the area of investigation is increased, and if this be sufficiently extended, they so nearly disappear altogether as to be unworthy of serious regard. Two familiar instances may be quoted of the application of these truths—the theory of probabilities, based on an accurate observation of gambling, in which luck is supposed to inhere; and the construction of life insurance tables, based upon calculations wide enough to reduce the proverbial uncertainty of life to an actual and negotiable commodity.

The word "statistics" was first employed in the middle of the last century by Professor Achenwall, of Göttingen, who is considered by some the founder of the science, but before his time separate branches of statistics had been ably treated by various writers. From an early date the "dismal science" had attracted the attention of the "gloomy English." Towards the close of the seventeenth and at the commencement of the eighteenth century Reynolds, Child, and Pretty published valuable information relating to the commerce, manufacture, and finance of this country. At a later period Price, Arthur Young, and Chalmers treated the subject of population with great ability. Young left a monument of his talent and industry in his various publications relating to agriculture, and Playfair's work on commerce has a high reputation. Within the space of a year the claims of John Howard, the philanthropist, to high rank as a statist have been eloquently advocated by Dr. Guy. Howard's fame as a philanthropist and martyr is deservedly so great that we are apt to overlook the means by which he succeeded in impressing an obdurate generation with the wrongs of prisoners. In 1773, when he was appointed Sheriff of Bedford, the prisons of this country were a disgrace to a nation with any pretension to civilization. Prisons were private property, and gaolers lived by fees levied with sublime impartiality on the innocent and on the guilty. In the same patient persevering spirit with which, seventeen years before, he liberated his fellow-captives in France, and reformed the treatment of prisoners of war, Howard set about improving the condition of the deplorable creatures then imprisoned in the "bridewells" of England. It is more than probable that had he contented himself with investigating one or two especially flagrant cases he might have succeeded in creating a "passing sensation," even in the languid public opinion of his day, but it is clearly impossible that a mere statement of a few aggravated cases would have had sufficient influence to stimulate legislative action. With the mind of a statist, as well as the heart of a philanthropist, he set about collecting that mass of evidence which produced the two Acts of 1774. He started on a new tour of inspection into the counties he had lately visited, and examining, not the bridewells only, but the houses of correction, and the city and town gaols, made acquaintance with the terrible gaol distemper, and its scarcely less formidable associate, confluent small-pox. Fortified by a mass of frightful details, he was prepared, the year after his shrievalty, to give that evidence before a Committee of the House of Commons which, by its tremendous accumulation and arrangement of facts, startled a horror-struck Legislature into immediate action. Complete inquiry, and the consequent number of facts, carried the day; and the victory which might have been denied to the philanthropist, was achieved with comparative ease by the statist, who, armed at all points, bore down opposition by sheer weight of evidence.

Strange to say, the success of the good man who achieved the greatest single-handed victory in the parliamentary history of England failed to awake the national mind to the value of method. Detached efforts were made from time to time, among which may be cited Sir John Sinclair's "Statistical Account of Scotland," and Colquhoun's "Treatise on the Wealth, Power, and Resources of the British Empire," but the systematic arrangement of facts required the magic imprint of the genius of generalization before it could take rank as a regular science.

This work of crystallizing scattered rows of figures into a solid science was performed by one great mind. On the 22nd of February, 1796, was born at Ghent, Adolphe Quetelet, who, after living to construct the Science of Statistics, died full of years and honour, in the corresponding month of the present year. At an early age he became Professor of Mathematics in his native town, and in 1820 was admitted to the Brussels Academy of Sciences and Letters, which, chiefly owing to his endeavours, expanded into the Royal Academy of Belgium. From an early period, he devoted himself to the study of numbers, and produced, at different times, works on the theory of probabilities, the *Statistique Criminelle* and the *Physique Morale*. In these famous works, which appeared before 1835, he announced opinions which astounded the world, but have since been amply verified by constant investigation. By a masterly application of the inductive system to moral and social problems, he educed, from a vast collection of isolated facts, generalizations which amazed the world of his day to the full as much as the conclusions of physical philosophers had startled and terrified preceding generations. Striking boldly at the barren province of metaphysical speculation, he reduced the most incomprehensible acts of human beings to a fixed law.

Immediately before the appearance of his great works the theories of Quetelet were bruited abroad, and the attention of the thinkers of England was awakened to the value of the new science that he had created. The British Association at once perceived the importance of figures scientifically handled, and suggested, with excellent insight, the formation of a society which should devote itself to the study of statistics. One of the earliest to identify himself with the movement was the veteran Malthus. This singularly clear and powerful thinker, who had startled, if not shocked, England a quarter of a century before by his able "Essay on the Principles of Population as it Affects the Future Improvement of Society," at once saw that he had lived long enough to encounter a generation capable of appreciating him. During the travels in which his early manhood was passed, he—struck by Hume's "Essay on the Populousness of Ancient Nations"—had perceived the importance of applying numbers as a test of historical truth. From remote periods vague statements had been made as to the vast multitudes of human beings subsisting in certain places, or wandering from spot to spot in the course of their periodical migrations. On testing the means of subsistence at the disposal of these peoples, many calculations, previously received with implicit faith, proved devoid of reasonable foundation. The application of the food test to ancient populations produced a similar effect to the application of chemistry to organic matter. From the materials at his disposal Malthus argued with irresistible logic, nor could he—when he anticipated the poverty of England, for the reason that the population increased in geometrical while the food-producing power of the country only increased in arithmetical progression—be expected to anticipate the enormous revolution destined to be brought about by free trade, and increased facilities for communication.

Perceiving at once the potency of a science which fused scattered and apparently discordant elements into one harmonious whole, Charles Babbage, the famous inventor of the calculating machine, threw himself warmly into the project for founding the new society. Impressed with the idea that what formerly had been done by the unaided work of human brains could be accomplished by machinery, he had devoted not only a great part of his valuable life, but £20,000 of his own money, to the perfection of the remarkable engine which bears his name. At this time at the zenith of his fame, he perceived, with that broadness of view which so eminently characterized him, the importance of the budget of facts which Quetelet had communicated to the British Association, and for which no place could be found in any section. At the instance of Babbage, the committee of the Statistical Section of the British Association met at his house, and at once determined on the establishment of a society devoted to the collection and elaboration of Statistics alone.

On the 15th March, 1834, was founded the Statistical Society of London, for the purpose of procuring, arranging, and publishing "Facts calculated to illustrate the condition and prospects of society." The Statistical Society considered it to be the first and most essential rule of its conduct to exclude carefully all opinions from its transactions and publications, to confine its attention rigorously to facts, and, as far as might be found possible, to facts stated numerically and arranged in tables. By the provisional committee —composed of Henry Hallam, Charles Babbage, Richard Jones, and John Elliot Drinkwater—was endorsed the opinion previously expressed by the Statistical Section of the British Association at Cambridge—that the whole subject admitted a division into four great classes—(1) economical statistics; (2) political statistics; (3) medical statistics; (4) moral and intellectual statistics. Further analysis revealed that—

Economical statistics comprehend—(1) the statistics of the natural productions and the agriculture of nations; (2) of manufacture; (3) of commerce and currency; (4) of the distribution of wealth, or all facts relating to rent, wages, and profits, etc.

Political statistics furnish three subdivisions—(1) the facts relating to the elements of political institutions, the number of electors, jurors, etc.; (2) legal statistics; (3) the statistics of finance and of national expenditure, and of civil and military establishments.

Medical statistics, strictly so called, require at least two subdivisions, and the great subject of population may also be conveniently classed as a subdivision of medical statistics.

Moral and intellectual statistics were held to include —(1) the statistics of literature; (2) of education; (3) of religious instruction and ecclesiastical institutions; (4) of crime.

To these four great divisions and their fourteen subdivisions the various departments of statistics were declared to be referrible, but it is also stated that in all probability more would be required.

The provisional committee, who did their work in a style worthy of their great reputation, added to the analysis just quoted a large number of valuable suggestions, which have all been adopted from time to time by Fellows of the Society. It was recommended that immediate communication should be opened with the statistical department established by Government at the Board of Trade. Inquiry was to be stimulated both at home and abroad, and relations were to be cultivated with all societies having objects bearing upon statistical research. It was suggested that not only new, but old statistics might advantageously be collected, arranged, condensed, and published. The archives of the East India Company were indicated as a storehouse whence immense quantities of valuable material might be drawn, and the pursuit of statistics in the Colonies and other countries, wherein society was starting from a *tabula rasa*, was warmly recommended.

The work of the Society being thus somewhat limited and defined, the committee proceeded to consider the best means, firstly, of collecting fresh statistical information, and secondly of arranging, condensing, and publishing that already in existence. On the method of collecting information, the committee expressed itself in the following luminous and suggestive paragraph:—"Towards collecting fresh statistical information, the first step, in order both of time and importance, would be the arrangement of a good set of interrogatories, to be drawn up under the superintendence of the sub-committees, and afterwards examined, sanctioned, and circulated by the Council.

The careful execution of this task is essential, both to afford guidance and aid to individual inquiries and to protect the Society against the influx of imperfect or irrelevant statements. Willing agents of inquiry exist in abundance quite ready to aid in collecting materials; but few of these agents take a very wide view of all the objects of statistical inquiry, and indeed few have very distinct notions about the precise information the Society may wish to collect, even as to any one object. To sketch, therefore, by means of interrogatories carefully and succinctly drawn, the whole outlines which it is wished to fill up, is the only way to secure to the Society the full benefit to be expected from their zeal. It is difficult to overrate the importance of the step which will be made towards the accumulation of statistical knowledge from all quarters of the globe, by the publication of such a set of questions; but the operation will be as laborious as it is important. It properly may, and probably will, form the chief object of the exertions of the Council during the first year of the Society's existence."

Immediately on its foundation the Society presented an imposing appearance, due not only to the number —398—of original Fellows, but to the important names figuring on the list. The Marquis of Lansdowne was the first president; Lord Fitzwilliam, Lord Sandon, Sir Charles Lemon, and Lieutenant-Colonel

Sykes, vice-presidents; the immortal historian of the Middle Ages figured as treasurer, and Messrs. Drinkwater, Greig, and Maclean as secretaries. Among the Council are the names of Charles Babbage, John Buckle, the Bishop of London (Blomfield), Samuel Jones Lloyd (afterwards Lord Overstone), G. R. Porter, John Tidd Pratt, George Poulett Scrope, Nassau Senior, Thomas Tooke, and William Whewell. One foreign Fellow only appears on the first list of the Statistical Society, but this one was no other than the illustrious Adolphe Quetelet. Many names which were at that time, or have since become, famous, follow those great pioneers of statistical science. Among these may be cited the late Baron Alderson, Richard Bethell (afterwards Lord Westbury), the late Lord Brougham, Mark Isambard Brunel (afterwards knighted), I. K. Brunel—the champion of the broad-gauge, and designer of the *Great Eastern* steamship—John Bonham Carter, Edwin Chadwick, Francis Chantrey, the late Lord Denman, William Ewart Gladstone, George Grote, Joseph Hume, Charles Knight, Lord Jeffrey, Charles Shaw Lefevre, J. R. McCulloch, Sir Francis Palgrave, the late Baron Parke, John Murray, Ashurst Majendie, Lord Minto, Sir Harris Nicolas, Sylvain Van de Weyer, R. Vernon Smith, M. Ricardo, Lord John (now Earl) Russell, Henry Ker Seymer, and the Duke of Somerset.

In addition to a long roll of remarkable men, the Statistical Society now numbers among its Fellows two most distinguished ladies—whom, in despite of custom and prejudice, it has deemed worthy of election. The names of Florence Nightingale and of the Baroness Burdett Coutts add no small lustre to the Society, which has by their election vindicated its claim to stand foremost in the van of progress.

As might have been expected, a body backed by a superabundance of brain power increased rapidly in numbers and importance. The labours of Quetelet cast a halo of glory about the new Society, and the steady toil of its members supplied admirable papers and discussions. Throughout the whole course of an eminently successful career the Society has never sought either Government subsidy or Royal patronage, except in the case of the late Prince Consort, himself a pupil of Quetelet. Following the steps of his illustrious father, His Royal Highness the Prince of Wales is now the Honorary President of the Society, the actual presidential chair having been recently occupied by Lord Houghton, Mr. Gladstone, Mr. Newmarch, and Dr. Farr. At the present moment this dignified position is admirably filled by Dr. Guy. Owing to the independent attitude of the Society it has never been incorporated by Royal Charter, and does not enjoy, like many learned bodies, the advantage of sumptuous apartments in Burlington House. Not long since the Society, feeling crippled in its narrow precincts in St. James's Square, set on foot a project for building a stately edifice at Westminster, to form a home for learned societies, but so many of these have found accommodation at Burlington House, that the "Statistical" is left almost alone in its glory, and has migrated from St. James's Square in company with its faithful ally, the "Institute of Actuaries," to the house in King's College recently vacated by the principal of the College, Canon Barry. The last session was marked by the action of the Council in giving effect to the views of the President, Dr. Guy, regarding John Howard and his claim to be considered as much a statist as a philanthropist, by establishing the Howard medal—a bronze trophy—to be given every year to the author of the best essay on some subject in social statistics.

The subject of the essay for which the medal will be given in 1874 (the centenary of the year in which Howard achieved his parliamentary triumph) is "The State of Prisons, and the Condition and Treatment of Prisoners in the Prisons of England and Wales, during the last half of the eighteenth century, as set forth in Howard's 'State of Prisons,' and his work on 'Lazarettos.'"

The subject for 1875 is "The State of the Dwellings of the Poor in the Rural Districts of England, with special regard to the improvements that have been made since the middle of the eighteenth century, and their influence on the health and morals of their inmates."

The "Proceedings" are embodied in the *Journal of the Statistical Society*, where also are found papers read at important gatherings, such as statistical congresses, and at the annual meeting of the British Association. Obituary notices and reviews are also included in the Journal, which on great occasions, such as that of the discussion on the Purchase of Railways by the State, requires the addition of an extra number.

In addition to this famous argument, which occupied three entire evenings, many interesting subjects have been discussed during the past two years, among which may be mentioned the price of coal, the recent progress of national debts, the statistics of legal procedure in England, the Bengal census, the income and property tax, the statistics of suicide among British troops, the elections of 1868 and 1874, local government, and co-operative land societies. At the discussion on the Purchase of Railways by the State, it was my good fortune to be present. For three successive Tuesdays the old room in St. James's Square was crowded to excess. Crammed together in a stifling atmosphere—suggesting that philosophers, however much they may care for sanitary laws when applied to the masses, are indifferent to them so far as they personally are concerned—the statists fought the great battle between Imperialism and private enterprise. An admirable paper by Mr. Biddulph Martin, advocating the propriety of the State purchase of Railways, was the apple of discord thrown among the great authorities present. The Imperial theory was supported by Captain Tyler, and ably contested by Mr. William Newmarch, who vigorously opposed the scheme on purely financial grounds, and declared that the value, or rather the prospective value, of English Railways had been grossly underrated at six hundred millions, and that a thousand millions would more accurately represent the sum the country would be called upon to pay for the privilege of becoming its own carrier. On this memorable evening the discordant estimates of rival statists filled the souls of visitors with amazement. Millions—ay, hundreds of millions—flew about the room like the "chunks of old red sandstone" at the famous meeting of the Geological Society on the banks of "the Stanislow." At the last meeting on this great subject Mr. Allport, the veteran manager of the Midland Railway, distinguished himself by a horse, foot, and artillery attack upon the theorists who propounded uniform fares, and was combated with equal ability by Mr. Hammond Chubb, who, in a vigorous speech, revived the falling fortunes of the Imperial Rule of the Road. In the hands of these learned gentlemen enormous sums were manipulated with such extraordinary facility that I became abashed at my own insignificance, and on reaching the cool air of St. James's Square found myself unable to bring my mind down from the contemplation of millions to the consideration of a humble cab-fare. I verily believe that cabby got much the better of me on that memorable evening from my inability to reduce my calculating power to the level of sixpences.

But the lively and pleasant, if stuffy, evenings in the old room are over now, for the Society is well bestowed in its new dwelling by the banks of the Thames almost within speaking distance of the Registrar-General, and within a stone's-throw of the old haunts of the Royal Academy, and of the Royal and other Scientific Societies which now find shelter in Burlington House. The rapidly-increasing number of Fellows has long demanded increased accommodation, and the Society has at last acquired ample scope for its lively debates—in connection with which I will add only one aspiration,—that when the members again discuss a subject with the animation, vigour, and skill expended on the Railways, may I be there to see, to hear, and to learn.

XIV.

THE ROYAL GEOGRAPHICAL SOCIETY.

The study of geography has been pursued at various epochs from very different motives. Love of adventure —in other words, the hope of getting something or of escaping from a condition too grievous to be endured— was doubtless the parent of geographical science, the observations and itineraries of those who travelled for piratical or other purposes being gradually systematized by map-makers and cosmogonists. From the earliest periods theories of the universe existed, most of which were abolished as bit by bit the true figure of the globe was revealed. Perhaps this perpetual destruction of old and construction of new systems formed one of the chief fascinations of geography in the many centuries during which mankind was occupied in chasing the Unknown from the face of the earth. At the present moment little remains to be discovered and described—as, excepting the polar regions, Central Asia, Inner Brazil, Central Africa, Australia, and the islands of Borneo and Madagascar, the world is depicted and understood with a very fair approach to accuracy.

It was not always so—and there are few more instructive and humiliating occupations than that of comparing the cosmogonies and geographical systems of various periods. In one particular the most ancient world-systems agree. The world was a flat disc or a parallelogram, surrounded on all sides by the ocean, from beyond which sprang the vast blue dome of the heavens. To the Chaldean shepherd, living and dying within fifty or a hundred miles of one central spot, or to the early Greek voyager, who thought a trip to the Black Sea a desperate undertaking, there was little either in the earth beneath his feet or in the azure vault overhead to indicate that the world was of globular form. To him, then, the earth was shield-like, with the ocean stream representing a rim—the whole being surmounted by a canopy; or, in other words, the world was a circle of earth, more or less raised in the centre, and covered by a crystal tent, around which flowed a moat. In the centre of this world was either the abode of the primæval geographer or the chief seat of divine worship. Thus Olympus, and at a later date Delphi, were the Greek centres of the world, and geographers of the Middle Ages invariably place Jerusalem in the centre of their curious maps. Homer, like many of his successors, never dreamt of a spherical world, but imagined it to be a flat circular body, round which flowed the ocean stream; while over it, resting on Caucasus and Atlas, stretched the heavenly dome. This conception becomes more intelligible when we recollect that the world of Homer did not extend beyond the Mediterranean, the Caspian Sea, the Red Sea, and the Persian Gulf. Out of ocean, or perhaps rather on the other side of its stream, the sun rose in the morning and sank at eve, and the two points where it appeared to touch the water formed the cardinal points in Homeric geography; the world being thus divided into halves, one towards the rising and the other towards the setting sun. Far to the west—beyond the setting sun and across the ocean stream—were the shadowy realms of Hades, while under the earth were the regions of Tartarus, the abode of punished gods. A glance at a map will show that Hellas is the centre of the countries enumerated by Homer.

At a later date—the comforting conclusion that the temple at Olympus was the centre of the world, and, therefore, of the universe, received many shocks. The well-known attempt of the Phœnicians to circumnavigate Libya, the voyage of Hanno, and the expedition of Scylax, had opened the minds of men to the possibility of the world being something more than a mere fringe around the Mediterranean, and the extensive commerce of the Ionian cities had served to explode mythical accounts of the earth's form and extent, and to prepare the way for more rational, though hardly more correct, theories. To Thales of Miletus is ascribed the introduction of scientific geography. He is said by some to have asserted the sphericity of the earth, but others describe this theory of sphericity as applied to the universe rather than to the world. Thus, according to Thales, the heaven was a hollow ball, in the midst of which the earth, in form like a tambourine, floated, as a cork floats in water, or rather, as the yolk of an egg is contained within the white and the shell. Anaximander was also of opinion that the earth was cylindrical in form, and neither he nor any philosopher of the Ionian school appears to have had any inkling of the spherical form of the earth. The origin of the spherical doctrine can be clearly traced to the Pythagoreans, who derived the idea from astronomical observations, and their views obtained general acceptance by the time of Plato. To Pythagoras himself has been frequently ascribed the idea of a pyrocentric Kosmos—with worlds revolving round a central sun—according to the Copernican, or, to speak more accurately, the Newtonian scheme.

Be this as it may, the belief that the world is only one of many planets made no progress in the ancient world. It was far more consonant with the dignity of man to place his abode in the centre of the universe, and to make all things subsidiary to his honour and comfort.

Herodotus inclined towards none of these views, and seems to have preferred the Xenophantic theory that the world is at the bottom of the universe, firmly rooted in infinite space. The extent of country visited and described by the most important of ancient travellers induced him to ridicule the idea that the world was circular. According to him it would be rather of an oval shape, having its extension east and west, surrounded, in all probability, by water like a huge island. In justice to Herodotus it may be observed that this plan of the world exactly coincided with his experience, the known world being longer from east to west than from north to south. This oval or oblong theory received a great accession of strength from the conquests of Alexander in the east, and the expedition of Pytheus of Massilia to the north-west coasts of Europe. This famous voyager followed the coasts of Spain and Gaul, passed up the British Channel, and thence along the east coast of England and across the Northern Ocean to Thule.

While the dimensions of the known world were thus

rapidly expanding, philosophy was paving the way for a more correct and scientific system of geography. Pythagoras, or his followers, and at a later date Plato and Aristotle, perceived the spherical form of the earth, and subsequent observations confirmed the truth of this important discovery; but, oddly enough, the Epicureans still adhered to the primitive notion of a shield. Towards the end of the third century B.C., Eratosthenes of Cyrene raised geography to the dignity of a science. He constructed maps on mathematical principles, and invented parallels of latitude and longitude. He taught that the earth was spherical in form, surrounded by a firmament of similar shape, both of which revolved about one and the same axis. He also performed the feat of measuring the circumference of the earth by an ingenious method. He ascertained by astronomical observation that the arc between Alexandria and Syene was 1-50th part of the earth's circumference; he then measured the distance between these two places, and found it to be 5000 stades, whence the total circumference would be 250,000 stades, or 28,800 miles. His method was correct, but some inaccuracy in his observations involved an error of nearly 4,000 miles. Dividing the earth into the Northern and Southern Hemispheres by the imaginary line called the Equator, he proceeded to draw eight parallels of latitude at unequal intervals. These parallels were crossed at right angles by seven meridians. Considering that only a portion of the northern hemisphere was inhabited, equal in extent to one-eighth of the globe's surface, he compared the plan of the habitable world to a Macedonian *chlamys*. From the days of Eratosthenes to those of Strabo and Pliny, no very great advance was made in geographical science. By the Romans the philosophical was neglected for the practical element, both Pomponius Mela and Pliny giving a very good account of the countries with which they were acquainted, and only falling back on "fancy geography," sphynxes and griffins, when touching the borderland of the Unknown.

Ancient geography was destined to attain its highest perfection under Claudius Ptolemy, an Alexandrian philosopher of the second century after Christ, and to his influence the blundering geography of the Middle Ages is often unjustly assigned. Ptolemy does not claim the merit of originating a system of geography, but amply acknowledges his obligation to Marinus of Tyre, whose writings are embodied in the work of the Alexandrian. The latitude and longitude of famous places was arrived at with greater certainty, and Ptolemy further improved his maps by drawing his parallels of latitude and meridians of longitude at equal intervals—a great advance on the system of

Eratosthenes. Further improvements were also made by drawing the meridians, not in parallel but converging lines, and in adding parallels of latitude south of the equator. So far, then, had the science of geography advanced, under Ptolemy—a spherical world formed the centre of the universe, and around it revolved, in their crystal spheres, the sun, moon, and *ignes minores*. The globe had been divided in two by the equator, and equal parallels of latitude and meridians of longitude had been laid down. The outlines of Europe had been ascertained with tolerable accuracy, and the greater part of Asia and Africa roughly sketched out.

So far geography had steadily, if slowly, advanced, but a period had now arrived when that and every other science—together with art and literature—were doomed to be arrested by an extraordinary determination of the human mind towards theology, to the exclusion of all positive studies. For nearly eight hundred years the human intellect was plunged in utter night. What little mental activity existed was exerted in one particular direction, and the adventures of an illiterate friar or the insane ravings of an unwashed recluse were considered more worthy of record and criticism than the observations of travellers or the deductions of mathematicians. The discourses of Roman orators and Grecian sages were ignominiously expunged from the parchment required for miraculous biographies and apocryphal histories. That this peculiar phase of superstition should have seized upon barbarians was perhaps not to be wondered at, but the enslavement of the Greek mind will ever present a melancholy problem to the student of psychology.

The effect on geography of this eclipse of the human understanding was immediate and complete. Within three hundred years of the death of Ptolemy his system had fallen into general discredit, and the spherical theory of the earth was sneered at as ridiculous and condemned as blasphemous. Curious maps appeared, in which all the errors of the most ancient systems were reproduced, and the world was held to be a mountain surrounded by water, situated at the bottom of the universe, and shut in by crystal walls and a crystal vault, or double heaven. With logic unanswerable in the sixth century it was urged that if the world were not the base and centre of the universe it would fall down, and the idea of a globe inhabited by antipodes was demonstrated to be as absurd as it was impious. From the maps of this and several succeeding centuries all traces of equator, parallels, and meridians disappeared. The world was an oblong hill, round which flowed the ocean, and the ancient fallacy that the Caspian Sea was an inlet of the ocean was revived. Men went back to original conceptions, and despising the experience and thought of ages as mere heathen learning, disdained to encumber themselves with facts.

The site of the terrestrial paradise was an enormous difficulty, and the course of the four rivers which flowed from it also exercised the ingenuity of mediæval geographers. It is impossible to refrain from sympathizing with these martyrs to science and superstition. They were bound, on pain of fire and faggot, to find a place on their maps for the terrestrial paradise, and in their despair "dashed it in" somewhere. Paradise was sometimes beyond the ocean altogether, but this theory involved the expedient of conducting the four rivers under the ocean stream, and was abandoned in favour of a more eligible site in the highest part of the world. Sometimes this is in Central Asia, sometimes in Armenia, and occasionally in the fabled Mountains of the Moon, but is always described as an inaccessible spot. For some unexplained reason the oblong maps went out of fashion about the eleventh century, and were supplanted by the old shield-like circle surrounded by water, but now having Jerusalem instead of Delphi for the central point. Between this period and the end of the fourteenth century a great advance was made. The mariner's compass was invented, the astrolabe came into general use, the spherical form of the earth was insisted on by Mandeville, and the map of Marino Sanuto and the famous Carte Catalane were produced.

While the East was becoming daily better known by the travels of Marco Polo, Rubruquis, and Mandeville, the Portuguese and Spaniards were fighting the Moors in the West, but it was not till 1418 that the capture and colonization of the Canaries prepared the way for the circumnavigation of Africa. Dim traditions of ancient voyages around Libya had reached Prince Henry of Portugal, and a great impulse was given to African exploration. Bit by bit the west coast was explored, until, standing southward, and being driven eastward by heavy gales, Bartholomew Diaz rounded the Cape of Good Hope and came to in Delagoa Bay, an exploit followed by the successful voyage of Vasco de Gama round the Cape to India. Pending this expedition Christopher Columbus made the most important geographical discovery of ancient or modern times. Columbus was not only a practical sailor, but a skilled theoretical geographer, and found much employment at Lisbon in making maps and globes for the Portuguese expeditions. Believing in the reported great extension of Asia to the eastward, and believing also the world to be much smaller than it really is, the great Genoese thought that he had only to sail across an island-studded ocean to reach the empires of Chipangu and Cathay. In most of the maps of the period immediately preceding that of Columbus, islands are laid down, but no idea of another continent had occurred to any one. Nothing can be more ridiculous than the attempt to ascribe the discoveries of Columbus to "information received" from the Northmen during a supposed voyage to Iceland. On the contrary, he firmly believed that the first continent he came to would be Eastern Asia, or rather Japan. The state of knowledge at his time fully warranted this belief. Ptolemy, whose works appear to have been preserved from utter loss by the Arabs, had extended Asia far to the eastward of its proper position, and the discovery of countries beyond the India known to him had brought the eastern coasts of Asia, as described by Marco Polo, still further eastward of their real longitude; and as Chipangu was represented to be 1500 miles distant from the mainland, it is not to be wondered at that on a globe of the fifteenth century the east coast of Japan is placed within seventy degrees of the Azores, and "India beyond the Ganges" within ninety, instead of at more than double those distances. The persistence with which Columbus clung to the idea that he had all along been navigating in an ocean full of islands is proved by the declaration made by him just before his fourth voyage

—that the passage westward to the Indies lay between the lands discovered by him in his second and third voyages.

The history of American discovery induces the feeling often arrived at by those who study the history of great inventions and discoveries—that if Columbus had not discovered the Western world just when he did, somebody else would have been before him, as Vespucci trod upon his heels. The reassertion of the spherical form of the earth was the real cause of the great outbreak of marine exploration. The revival of this important truth set mariners to planning the circumnavigation of the earth in good earnest. Thus Columbus and Cabot both pursued independent investigations, and arrived at the same conclusion respecting the propinquity of India, but in the magnitude of their new discoveries ultimately lost sight of their original design. These two great Italian navigators drew their inspiration from pure science, acted on their knowledge of the sphere, and calculated the effect of great circle sailing.

After this date the most distant seas were furrowed by European keels. Spain, Portugal, France, and England vied with each other in pushing into strange countries, and while the literature of travel received many rich additions, the Eastern and Western worlds were rapidly mapped out. England was conspicuous by her endeavours to discover a north-west or north-east passage to India, and has during the last 300 years expended much money and many lives in a pursuit which has hitherto proved barren. Meanwhile the less scientific than practical men of Devon sailed forth in tall ships, and enlivened the pursuit of geographical knowledge by leading the Spaniards a terrible life. Hawkins, Drake, Oxenham, and Frobisher had a keen eye for a Spanish galleon, and enriched the records of maritime discovery and themselves at the same time. From that to the present time the progress made has no longer been so brilliant, for the simple reason that there was so much less to discover, although the voyages of Cook, Tasman, and La Perouse disclosed islands and continents where their existence had been previously undreamt of.

For about a century and three-quarters after its incorporation the Royal Society was, with the exception of its early offshoot, the Royal Astronomical Society, the only body which gave a scientific impulse to geographical investigation. At rare intervals, and in a grudging, half-hearted, reluctant way, the State —I cannot say, "came forward," but allowed to be extracted from its coffers a small sum of money—generally ridiculously inadequate to the purpose for which it was intended. When a grant was made the usual practice was to confide its administration to a special committee of the Royal Society, who thus to a considerable extent regulated the distribution of such crumbs as were occasionally thrown to science. Even at such a recent date as 1830 the claims of science and scientific men received scant recognition in this country, and while the *savans* of France and Germany were decorated with endless stars, crosses, and ribands, and sate familiarly at the table of kings, our own philosophers were contemptuously neglected by a nation caring for nothing but politics, religion, and commerce. Thanks, however, to the exertions of Brewster and Babbage, and in a considerable degree to the spirited advocacy of Brougham, the British mind became aware that an attitude of indifference towards science was indicative of a barbarous nation. An immediate and permanent reaction took place, and the fashionable taste for science—first developed by Davy—soon assumed serious proportions, while the exertions of Birkbeck contributed to spread a taste for physical science among the great body of the people. At this period of transition in popular feeling three bodies sprang into existence, all of which have since exercised an important influence upon scientific research. These were the British Association for the Advancement of Science, the Statistical Society, its immediate outgrowth, and the Royal Geographical Society.

The latter important organization, in common with the Geographical and Kosmos Clubs, is the offspring of the Raleigh Travellers Club, the idea of which was first suggested by Captain Arthur de Capell Brooke to Captain Mangles, R.N., Lieutenant Holman, the famous blind traveller, Colonel Leake, and Mr. Leigh in the autumn of 1826. Great quaintness characterized the original plan. The club was to consist of eighty-five members, and the globe was to be mapped out into divisions corresponding to the number of members, so that each division should be represented by a member, and the club collectively have visited every known part of the globe. Captain Brooke addressed a circular letter to the most distinguished travellers of the day, and the originators of the movement, joined by Mr. John Rennie, Mr. C. R. Cockerill, and Captain Corry, R.N., held their first dinner at Grillon's Hotel. At the second meeting the name of "The Raleigh" was adopted by the club, and thenceforward its regular meetings were held at the Thatched House until its dissolution in 1854. New members came in rapidly. Eastern travellers were represented by Mr. Colebrooke, Mr. Marsden, and Mr. Baillie Fraser; African, South American, and European wanderers by Captain Cochrane, R.N. (afterwards Earl Dundonald), Mr. John Cam Hobhouse, and Mr. J. Rennie; surveyors, by Captain Owens, R.N.; and the bold explorers of the

Arctic Regions, by Sabine and Brooke, Parry and Franklin. Sir John Barrow also joined the club shortly after its inauguration, and presided at the second and third dinners. The second meeting, in 1827, was presided over by Mr. Marsden, author of that excellent edition of Marco Polo which rehabilitated the great traveller's reputation, and preceded the thoughtful edition of M. Pauthier and the elaborate and exhaustive work of Colonel Yule. On this occasion, Captain Brooke proposed that a permanent union should be established between geography and gastronomy, and that to this end members should be invited to present any scarce foreign game, fruits, fish, wines, etc., as a means of adding to the interest of the dinners, "not merely from the objects of luxury thus afforded, but for the observations they will be the means of giving rise to." This was successfully carried into effect—the members on various occasions discussing haunches of reindeer venison from Spitzbergen, Swedish brandy, rye-cake baked at the North Cape, Norway cheese, cloudberries from Lapland, Heshbon bread from the Dead Sea, capercailzie from Sweden, and hams from Mexico.

After extending hospitality for many years to all distinguished travellers, "dining and wining" Ross, from the North; Chesney, from the Euphrates; D'Abbadie, from Abyssinia; Vigne, from Cashmere;

Schomburgk, from Guiana; Wellsted, from Arabia; and Captain Shakespeare, from Asia; the Raleigh Club was dissolved in 1854, in order that a new club might be formed in closer connection with the Royal Geographical Society.

This child of the old Raleigh Dining Club was born on the 24th of May, 1830, when a numerous meeting took place at the Thatched House. The gathering was not confined to the members of the club, but was attended by many other gentlemen of a scientific turn, and the chair was taken by Mr. (afterwards Sir John) Barrow. It was then stated that among numerous literary and scientific societies established in the metropolis, one at least was wanting to complete the circle of scientific institutions, whose sole object should be the promotion and diffusion of that important and entertaining branch of knowledge — geography. The interest excited by this department of science was universally felt, and its advantages to mankind in general, and to a maritime nation like Great Britain, were at once acknowledged. To promote geographical investigation a Society was formed with the several objects of collecting, registering, digesting, and printing, for the use of the members and the public, in a cheap form and at certain intervals, any new and interesting facts which might come into the possession of the Society. The

Royal Geographical Society proposed also to accumulate a library of the best books on geography, and a complete collection of maps and charts from the earliest period of rude geographical delineation to the present time. It was also proposed to open communication with all literary and scientific societies whose objects include or sympathize with geography, and it was "hoped" that the Society would ultimately be enabled from its funds to render pecuniary assistance to such travellers as might require it, in order to facilitate the attainment of some particular object of research. At a meeting of the young Society, held at the rooms of the Horticultural Society in the following July, it was announced that in the short intervening time 400 members had been enrolled, and an enlarged programme was presented embracing almost every variety of geographical knowledge. It was urged, and with much good sense, that the age of great discoveries was nearly—if not quite—past, and that minute exactitude must for the future take the place of brilliant conception and daring adventure. Sir John Barrow quoted, and enlarged upon the quotation, "that the man who points out, in the midst of the wide ocean, a single rock unknown before is a benefactor of the human race."

The progress of the Society was rapid. In 1832, King William had been secured as Patron; the late

Duke of Sussex as Vice-Patron; and Lord Goderich as President. Five hundred and thirty-five members were enrolled, and beyond this number was an illustrious roll of foreign honorary members, among whom shines conspicuously the name of Alexander Von Humboldt. Encouraged by the receipt of £4495 in the first year, and a probable income of £1200 a year at least, the Council proceeded at once to publish a *Journal*—to be presented gratuitously to members—in addition to the "Proceedings," which are sent to every member within the United Kingdom. The Royal Patron had, moreover, encouraged the Society by a donation of fifty guineas, and some 400 volumes—the nucleus of the present splendid library—were presented to the Society by a few members. The Royal Geographical Society now began to assist discoverers with grants, and to reward them with premiums. The first premium was awarded to the unfortunate Richard Lander—one of those adventurous travellers who have fallen sacrifices to the object of penetrating Central Africa—and a subsidy was granted to the Arctic Expedition, conducted by Captain Back, in search of Captain Ross. Schomburgk's Guiana Expedition also received great assistance from the Society.

In 1834 the Royal premium was awarded to Lieutenant Alexander Burnes, afterwards murdered, with Sir William MacNaghten, by Akhbar Khan at

Kabul—"for having navigated the Indus, and communicated much new and important information regarding that river; for important observations made in a route *hitherto unknown to Europeans*, from Kabul, across the *Indian Caucasus*, to the ancient cities of Balkh and Bokhara; for new and interesting information regarding the upper course of the Oxus," etc. etc. During the next year the Council, encouraged by the flourishing state of the finances, launched out boldly, and voted £500 towards the outfit and maintenance of the two expeditions already subsidized—the Land Arctic Expedition and the Quorra Expedition—and, moreover, laid siege to the late Lord Monteagle, then Secretary of State for the Colonies, with such excellent effect as to extract £1000 from the national purse. In 1836, the progress of an African Exploring Expedition from Delagoa Bay having been put a stop to by the outbreak of a Kaffir war, the Society devoted £900 to the Guiana Expedition. Grey's Australian Expedition was also patronised by the Society, and in 1838 an historical name turns up in its annals. Five hundred pounds were voted, in conjunction with the Society for the Promotion of Christian Knowledge, for an expedition to Kurdistan to look up the Nestorian Christians, who for many centuries had found homes in nooks and corners of Central Asia. The mission was conducted by Mr.

Ainsworth and by a Nestorian Christian—a certain Mr. Rassam—since the *teterrima causa* of the successful, but useless and costly, Abyssinian war. The attention of the Society now became again turned towards African exploration, and a small subsidy was voted to Dr. Beke to assist him in his investigations.

Having, during the first few years of its existence, given fair promise of an eminently useful career, the Society—between the years 1840 and 1848—lapsed into that inertness which occupies a certain part of the history of almost all societies. These institutions start vigorously, but after a while, from causes on which it is unnecessary to dilate, sink into dulness and insignificance, from which they require to be aroused by the touch of a master hand. The sudden improvement in the income of the Society—which rose from £696 10*s*. 5*d*. in 1848 to £2584 7*s*. in 1855—was due mainly to the new life infused into the Society by Admiral Smyth, whose presidency was followed by the active reign of Sir Roderick Murchison, while the efforts of these invaluable presidents were ably seconded by Dr. Norton Shaw, at that time secretary of the Society. From a miserably low ebb the finances, which had been heavily drawn upon by the questionable policy of starting original expeditions, were restored to a healthy condition. Owing to the energetic advocacy of Sir Roderick Murchison, whose distinguished rank as a geologist lent additional weight to his recommendations, and whose tact in offering the inducement of a public map-room had no slight influence on the negotiation, her Majesty's ministers felt justified, in 1854, in offering "to submit annually to Parliament, in the Civil Service Estimates, a grant of £500 to the Royal Geographical Society, to enable the Society to hire a house or rooms for its meetings, and for the deposit and exhibition of its maps, upon the distinct understanding that the Society will bind itself to provide a public hall or suitable rooms where every person from town or country may go free of charge to obtain the information he might require." Their lordships also required that in making the annual application for the grant, the Society should furnish a short report of its proceedings, detailing the additions made to its maps or geographical knowledge, and specifying the number of persons who have visited the collections of the Society for the purpose of study or inspection during the preceding year—the report to be printed with the estimate laid annually before the House of Commons.

Under the presidency of Sir Roderick Murchison the Society first acquired that importance which it has since maintained and increased. The career of this remarkable man commenced in the army, but at the conclusion of the war in 1815 he—by the advice of Sir Humphry Davy—turned his attention to physical science. In 1825 he wrote his first geological paper, and from that time to his death was one of the most successful cultivators of geological science that this country has ever seen. His discovery of the "Silurian" system made his name famous, and his subsequent exposition of the Devonian, Permian, and Laurentian systems confirmed and increased his reputation. He was proud of his share in founding the Royal Geographical Society in 1830, when, in conjunction with Mountstuart Elphinstone, the late Lord Broughton, and Robert Brown, he assisted in drawing up, under the guidance of Sir John Barrow, the laws by which the Society has since been governed. During the latter part of his life his history is the veritable history of the Society. From the year 1843, when he first occupied the presidential chair, he occupied it at intervals, but for the last nine years of his life his tenure of office was continuous. As I have already shown, the Society was much indebted to this distinguished philosopher, who immortalized himself by predicting, in 1844, the golden future of Australia. Murchison, who had then just returned from examining the Ural Mountains, was greatly impressed by the resemblance between their geological formation and that of the great

Australian chain, which had been reported on at about the same period by Count Strzelecki, and in his presidential address he expressed his surprise that the latter region had as yet offered no trace of auriferous veins — the fact being that gold had actually been discovered by the Count, but that the news had been suppressed by the advice of the governor, Sir George Gipps, who feared that "If he made known his discovery, the maintenance of discipline amongst the 45,000 convicts, which the Australian colonies then contained, might be almost impossible." Murchison, unaware of the true state of affairs, and pursuing independently his study of the geology of Australia, became at last convinced that gold must exist there, and expressed that conviction on three public occasions—in a memoir read before the British Association, in a lecture delivered at the British Institution, and finally, in an article in the *Quarterly Review* for 1850, entitled "Siberia and California." The operations of Mr. Hargreaves produced, in 1851, the realization of these profound views, and triumphantly vindicated their accuracy. After this date Murchison took a prominent part in stimulating Australian explorations, and at his suggestion several Australian travellers, among whom were Strzelecki, Sturt, Leichhardt, Macdonald Stuart, and O'Hara Burke, received honorary rewards from the Society, to which Murchison had the gratification of announcing, in his last address, that whereas, in 1830, nothing was known of Australia beyond a small area around Sydney, two-thirds of the continent are now occupied.

Far from restricting his sympathies to the antipodes, Murchison devoted great attention and strenuous advocacy to Arctic exploration and African discovery. His deepest sympathies were engaged in the famous, but ill-fated expedition under Sir John Franklin, and when the *Erebus* and *Terror* were lost sight of he made it the business of his life to ascertain their fate, until the voyage of the *Fox*, under Sir Leopold McClintock, in 1857, solved the painful mystery. With like vigour Murchison addressed himself to the great field of African discovery. Having at a very early period satisfied himself that the interior of the continent—instead of being a mere sandy desert, as depicted on the maps of the time—was an elevated plateau—giving rise to great rivers like the Zambesi, the Congo, and the Nile, which flowed to east, west, and north almost from a common centre—he encouraged and assisted to the utmost of his power that great band of African travellers who have succeeded in tearing away a great part of the veil which long shrouded the interior of the continent. The soundness of his conclusions was in this, as in the case of Australian gold, completely demonstrated, and entitles him to a place among those philosophers of the first rank, who, in addition to marvellous patience and accuracy in the collection and arrangement of materials, are endowed with that sublime spark of creative imagination which kindles dry isolated facts into the living fire of a great truth. Not only in geology and geography did Murchison distinguish himself, but rendered important service to the cause of general science by assisting to found the British Association, and in devoting much time and care to the proceedings of that learned body. He was also Director-General of the Museum of Practical Geology and Chief of the School of Mines, in which capacity he readily grasped the opportunity of introducing scientific training into the education of the working classes, and took an active part in the labours of the Commission on the coal resources of the country. In addition to the valuable assistance which he rendered the Royal Geographical Society in obtaining from the Government, in 1854, the grant of an annual subsidy, he gave active aid in obtaining, in 1859, the Royal Charter of Incorporation, and also originated the Bellot Testimonial Fund—an admirable instance of the readiness with which English geographers appreciate true merit, irrespective of national distinctions.

In the address delivered by Major-General Sir Henry C. Rawlinson, from the presidential chair of the Royal Geographical Society, on the 27th of May, 1872, the brilliant career of Murchison was alluded to in the following terms :—

"It has often been a reproach to the Government of this country that scientific services are, as a rule, so little regarded and so poorly rewarded ; but Murchison's career furnished a bright example to the contrary. He was knighted in 1846, was made a K.C.B. in 1863, and a baronet in 1866. From the other sovereigns of Europe he also received a shower of well-earned honours. By the Emperor of Russia he was made a Knight of the 2nd Class of St. Anne, and subsequently a Grand Cross of the same order, and also of that of St. Stanislaus ; and as these honours were conferred for services rendered to the Russian Government, he was graciously permitted to accept them, and to wear the crosses and insignia at the British Court. Orders were also conferred upon him by the sovereigns of Sweden, Denmark, Italy, and Brazil. A list, indeed, has been lately published of nineteen stars, crosses, and other emblems of distinction which belonged to Sir Roderick at the time of his decease, and which constitute, as has been said, 'the largest number of honorary decorations which, in modern times, have been awarded by crowned heads to any individual for purely scientific attainments.'

"By the public and scientific bodies of this country and of the continent he was further rewarded with a similar profusion of titles and honours. He was a D.C.L. of Oxford, LL.D. of Cambridge, and M.A. of Dublin. Of the Royal Society he was not only a Fellow, but also a Vice-President, and had further received from it the Copley Gold Medal. Amongst similar first-class scientific prizes, he had been awarded the Brisbane Gold Medal from Edinburgh, the Prix Cuvier from Paris, and the Wollaston Medal from the Geological Society of London. He was a member of the Academies of St. Petersburg, Berlin, Copenhagen, Brussels, Stockholm, and Turin, and a corresponding member of the Institute of France. At home, at the time of his death, he was Vice-President of the Geographical and Geological Societies, a trustee of the British Museum, of the Hunterian Museum, and of the British Association for the Advancement of Science, an honorary member of the Royal Society of Edinburgh and of the Royal Irish Academy, President of the Hakluyt Society, Fellow of the Linnean Society, and of many other scientific bodies."

Far less fortunate in obtaining recognition of his great services was Sir Paul Edmund de Strzelecki, whose life was from its outset entirely devoted to the pursuit of pure science. After discovering and bringing to the notice of the Colonial department the rich deposits of native copper in the Upper Lake region of Canada, he—at the earnest solicitation of Sir George Gipps, the Governor-General of New South Wales—devoted five years of his life to a systematic survey of that portion of New South Wales which extends from the 30 deg. to the 39 deg. of south latitude. The labour of this survey was very great.

He made—to use his own words—7000 miles on foot, and incurred an outlay of £5000. He prepared a geological map of New South Wales and of Van Diemen's Land, on the scale of one inch to the mile, which he was unable to take upon himself to publish in this country, from a disappointment in the recovery of funds for that purpose consequent on the premature death of Sir George Gipps. In addition to the discovery of gold, Count Strzelecki penetrated through a series of rugged and sterile defiles into the beautiful tract of country named by him "Gipps' Land," and in the course of this exploration was compelled to cut his way for twenty-six days through a zone of almost impenetrable scrub. Although the expedition had been undertaken at the express request of the Governor, under the condition that the "Colonial treasury should be associated with the enterprise, and defray half the expenses," and that, in the event of his researches tending to results likely to benefit the public, Sir George Gipps would "recommend her Majesty's Government to repay him all the outlay which he might be obliged to incur in his expedition," the count never received a shilling beyond some £400 subscribed by the Tasmanian public. Undismayed, however, by the scant recognition of his services by the Colonial and the Imperial Government, which confined its notice of him to the offer of an official position in the Colonies, he produced his work on the "Physical Geography of New South Wales and Van Diemen's Land." This work appeared in 1845, and at once placed the name of Count Strzelecki on the roll of distinguished geographers. Science, however, has to regret that he was soon called away from his labours as an author to undertake the relief of suffering humanity, as he accepted the self-imposed and self-remunerated mission of distributing, during a period of four years, from 1846 to 1850, amongst the famine-stricken peasantry of Ireland, the relief which the liberality of the British public had collected for them. During this period he left the question of the discovery of gold and his other claims to the course of events. Meanwhile, however, the discovery of the precious metal in New South Wales had oozed out, and later explorers not merely enriched themselves suddenly, but claimed the reward offered by the

Legislative Council of Sydney to the discoverer of gold. That reward, however, was not distributed until 1853, when the Legislative Council supported the proposal of the Executive Government of the colony that the sum of £5000 should be given to those who first published the discovery and taught the miners how to wash the gold, and not to him who first made the discovery and kept it secret at the express request of the Executive Government. Justice, however, was done to Count Strzelecki's scientific researches in the course of the debates of the Legislative Council in its sitting on 5th October, 1853, and his claim to the discovery of the gold-fields in 1839 was established beyond all dispute.

It is somewhat to be wondered at that, after the treatment he had received, he applied for, and obtained, in 1845, letters of naturalization as a British subject, for he must have been convinced that in this country, and at that period, science, like virtue, was its own reward. But his faith in England was destined to receive a certain justification, for tardy justice—so far as honour and glory were concerned—was meted out to him when, at the recommendation of Mr. Gladstone, he was made a Knight Commander of the order of St. Michael. From the time when Sir Roderick Murchison devoted his great powers to its consolidation and advancement, the Royal Geographical Society, gradually abandoning the policy of initiating expeditions, contented itself with making grants in aid of such enterprises, or in bestowing rewards upon brilliant and successful travellers. Large sums have been spent upon the library and the map-room; indeed, to the latter is now faithfully devoted the whole sum contributed to the Society by Government. It is perhaps not so well known as it deserves to be, that the map-room is now, and has since the annual £500 was first given, been thrown open to the public, who are free to inspect and in many cases to take tracings of the maps in possession of the Society. The country may therefore be congratulated on having laid out its five hundred a year to advantage, and on having for once gotten the best of a bargain. The map-room in the house at present occupied by the Society is 60 feet long by 40 feet broad, and is furnished with more than 60,000 maps. Perhaps it is as well that ordinary emigrants, travellers, and the general public are not aware of the privilege they may exercise on any day during office hours at the corner of Savile Row and Burlington Gardens; but the military and civil servants of Her Majesty well appreciate the value of the Society's map-room. No sooner does a squabble occur—in Ashanti, Abyssinia, or Atchin—than Government departments make a rush to Savile Row, and lay hands on all matter relating to that portion of the world which happens to be interesting for the moment.

With equally enlightened public spirit, the Royal Geographical Society offered, six years ago, gold and bronze medals to be competed for by public schoolboys, and the experiment has since been continued with very great success. A gold and a bronze medal are given to the first and second competitors in physical geography, and like prizes to those successful in political geography. These have been carried off by Eton College, Liverpool College, University College School, Clifton College, and the City of London School—among which the success of Liverpool College has been conspicuous. At the last examination, however, Liverpool did not carry off any of the prizes, while the City of London School took the gold medal for physical and the bronze medal for political geography.

Although possessing a handsome house of their own, worth some £20,000, the Fellows of the Society find it impossible to hold their general meetings, which take place on the two first Mondays in every month from November to June, within the limits of their own building. This is in part to be explained by the immense size to which the Society has grown, and in a considerable degree to the Royal Geographical Society being the "fashion." When a really genuine big lion returns from foreign wilds and is docile enough to "roar as gently as a sucking dove" at the bidding of the Council, a determined rush is made for admission, the lives of the Fellows are made weary unto them by the ladies of their acquaintance, and an immense audience thunders at the gate. Under these circumstances, the Chancellor and Senate of the University of London have—in a spirit of hearty liberality—permitted the Society to hold its meetings in their magnificent theatre at Burlington House. This permission was not granted by the University as a matter of course. On the contrary, the Senate were so outrageously worried by applications from various quarters to hold meetings in their hall, that they passed a resolution restricting its use to meetings connected with educational purposes, and it was considered a high compliment to the public importance and utility of the Royal Geographical Society, when that body was made an exception to the rule and permitted to make use of Burlington House for its meetings.

In addition to the privilege of attending meetings, listening to the great lions, and bearding the lesser lions during the discussion which follows the reading of papers, the Fellows have the use of a valuable library, containing 20,000 volumes on geography and cognate sciences, and a fine collection of English and foreign scientific periodicals. It would appear that the numerous Fellows avail themselves pretty thoroughly of their rights, for in the ten years ending in 1872 the rooms of the Royal Geographical Society were visited by 45,334 persons, and the evening meetings were attended by 55,300, making a total of 100,634 persons who have derived instruction or amusement from maps, books, and papers. No scientific society is in a more thoroughly healthy condition from a financial point of view, and none is acquiring new members more rapidly. In the report of the Council, read at the last anniversary meeting, it was announced that no fewer than 342 new members, besides nine honorary corresponding Associates, had been elected during the year. The total number now on the rolls is 2809 ordinary and seventy-six honorary corresponding members. The annual income of the Society is nearly £9000, and its capital, obtained from bequests and accumulations of subscriptions, amounts to about £25,000, partly invested in the freehold property in Savile Row and partly in public securities. During the last few years the library and the map-room have received many important additions. Valuable presents in books, and money for the purchase of them, have been made to the library; and, under the discriminating guidance of Mr. Keith Johnston, application was made to the Governments of Europe for the most important geographical documents which they have severally published. This appeal has been nobly responded to, more than 3500 sheets having been, during the past year, added to the collection of the Society, many of these being equally valuable as specimens of the most elaborate cartography and as indications of the latest geographical data. The *Journal of the Royal Geographical Society* has expanded into a bulky volume of valuable matter, admirably edited by the learned and indefatigable secretary, Mr. H. W. Bates, the value of whose labours has been handsomely acknowledged by Sir Henry C. Rawlinson, and by the Right Honourable Sir H. Bartle Frere, K.C.B. Disdaining—possibly overmuch—matter of purely antiquarian interest, and devoting itself rather to the development of present science than to the description and elucidation of exploded theories, the Royal Geographical Society has yet, among its wonderful collection of modern cartography, relics of the past, which cannot fail to interest the student of that extraordinary period when Europe was struggling through the twilight which followed the deep night of the Middle Ages. One of those is a *fac simile* of the extraordinary Mappa Mundi made by Richard of Haldingham, some time between 1275 and 1300, and preserved in Hereford Cathedral. This map is 52 inches in diameter, and is richly coloured. It is circular in form, the earth being surrounded by the ocean; the upper part of the map is the east, and in the centre is the city of Jerusalem. The Mediterranean Sea, with the Adriatic and Black Seas, occupies the lion's share of the map—which, it is needless to say, is entirely free from parallels or meridians. Far away to the north of the Black Sea is the Caspian—an inlet of the ocean—and the Red Sea and Persian Gulf are also shown, coloured a bright scarlet. There is little doubt that this map expresses exactly the state of mediæval geography at the close of the thirteenth century, for it could not be expected that the discoveries of Marco Polo would be immediately adopted by cartographers. The great rivers Nile and Danube are distinctly marked, with their many mouths opening to the sea, and the great cities are also put in with some approach to accuracy. Touching sacred or legendary sites no doubt is exhibited. The tower of Babel is boldly drawn, as are also the barns of Joseph, the labyrinth of Crete, the spot where the Israelites crossed the Red Sea, and the course of their wanderings in search of the promised land. Europe presents a curious outline. The Gulf of Lyons is completely filled up, and Spain more resembles a western prolongation of France than an independent peninsula; but the great rivers and the towns upon them are done justice to—the Rhone flows past Lyons to Marseilles—the Seine past Paris to the English Channel—the Thames from Oxford by London to the North Sea—the Severn by Worcester—and the Dee by Chester.

The British Islands present an odd outline, and suggest the idea they have undergone much squeezing to get them into the circle. On the opposite or eastern side, far beyond India, is a circular island containing four rivers. This is the terrestrial paradise with its central fountain whence flow the sweet waters of the earth. Adam and Eve are here represented, and a similar style of pictorial embellishment covers the whole of this marvellously interesting map. Mermaids disport in the seas, and the earth is tenanted by monoculi, acephali, and anthropophagi—strange races of men—and stranger birds and beasts, sphynxes, griffins, centaurs, dragons, the phœnix, and the salamander.

Of a later date than the Hereford map, but equally interesting to the geographer, is a model of the globe preserved in the library at Frankfort-on-the-Maine. Its date is supposed to be about 1520, and it affords a singularly accurate idea of the state of geographical knowledge shortly after the discovery of America. It is specially interesting, as showing the next stage of geography to that presented by the famous globe made at Nuremberg in 1492 by Martin Beham, in which it is supposed the islands are laid down in the same way as in the map used by Columbus in his first voyage. On Beham's globe three-fourths of the surface are occupied by the three continents then known—the Atlantic Ocean, the unknown American continent, and the Pacific Ocean being crowded into about 90 deg. of longitude. West of the Azores was the Island of Antilla, and to the south-west of the Cape de Verde Islands a large island marked: "In 585, Sir Brandon came here in his ship." Seventy degrees west of the Canaries lay Cipangi or Japan. In the twenty-eight years which elapsed between the discovery of America and the date of the Frankfort globe, the shape of the new continent had been partially made out, and the West Indies laid down with tolerable correctness. The Pacific side of the southern continent had also been sketched in; but the northern portion is only represented by an attenuated slip. In concurrence with preconceived ideas, Japan is placed just off the coast of Mexico, and the Northern Pacific is reduced to very narrow limits; but, perhaps, the most curious part of this globe is that which represents the Isthmus of Darien according to the ideas of Columbus himself, with a wide gap about the 10 deg. north latitude, affording ample passage for mariners to Japan, the Indies, and their fabulous wealth.

Interesting as are these memorials of early discoveries, the portraits and works of more recent geographers are endowed with even greater attraction. Around the Council Room of the Royal Geographical Society hang portraits of Sir John Barrow and Captain Richard Burton, of the gallant but ill-fated Lander, and the not less unfortunate Burnes, of Admiral Smyth, Dr. Kirk, Captain Speke, Dr. Livingstone, and other celebrated travellers; while in the place of honour is a noble marble bust of Murchison. It is impossible, however, to look on the walls thus tenanted without regretting that the period of the greatest prosperity and most brilliant development of the Society has been saddened by the death of many geographers of the first rank. During the last three or four years the names of Murchison and Strzelecki, Wood and Chesney, Keith Johnston and Arrowsmith, Maury and Sedgwick, McClure and Livingstone, have been added to the roll of the illustrious dead,—but albeit these great leaders of scientific inquiry have departed from the sphere of their labours, their spirit of earnest devotion to pure science—for its own sake—still animates those who, not unworthily, essay to fill the void they have left behind.

Printed by William Moore & Co.

www.ingramcontent.com/pod-product-compliance
Lightning Source LLC
LaVergne TN
LVHW010208110826
845151LV00002B/635
* 9 7 8 1 4 2 5 5 3 5 5 4 4 *